As They Went...

Experiencing God's Blessings Through Obedience

BY
KEVIN W. COSBY, D.MIN.

CHRISTOPHER
Books

As They Went...

By
Kevin W. Cosby, D.Min.

Printed in the United States of America

ISBN: 1-932203-21-4

Christopher Books
Louisville, Kentucky

Cover Illustration: Carolyn Wells, Mt. Juliet, Tennessee
Cover and Page Layout: Guardian Angel Communication Services, Nashville

DEDICATION

This work is dedicated to my father-in-law, Andrew Gholston Turner, who played an instrumental role in the development of my ministry during the early years. He often gave me his truck so that I could go to various speaking engagements. But most of all, he gave me the greatest gift of my life, his lovely daughter, Barnetta Turner.

Table of Contents

Introduction

There is an old story of Jewish origin about two angels who were sent to gather all of the prayers of the people on earth. One of the angels was assigned to gather all of the "Give me" petitions. The other angel was assigned the task of gathering all of the "Thank You" petitions. After a while, the angels returned to heaven. The angel assigned to collect the "Give me" prayers returned to heaven with bags overflowing. However, the angel assigned to gather the "Thank You" prayers returned with bags that were practically empty.

There is no way to tabulate what percentage of prayers to God are "Give me" prayers and what percentage are "Thank You" prayers. But, I'm very confident based on what I have observed in my own life and the lives of other Christians, that God receives more "Give me" prayers than "Thank You" prayers.

To illustrate my assertion, consider the familiar story of the ten lepers who cried to Jesus for mercy (Luke 17:11-19). The very word leprosy sent shivers through the ancient world. Although the term leprosy is used in the Bible to identify a number of dreaded skin diseases, generally, leprosy is understood as an incurable, infectious skin disease that covered its victims with scales and sores, and caused the limbs to deteriorate. Because of the highly contagious nature of the disease, lepers were forbidden to commingle with the rest of society. They were required to stand far off from other humans and, to alert passersby of their contagious condition, they had to cry, "Unclean! Unclean!" to warn uninfected, unsuspecting persons. Theirs was a life of exclusion, isolation, deterioration, and humiliation.

Jesus encountered the 10 lepers as He passed along the borders of Galilee and Samaria. The fact that Jesus was passing between these borders meant that the lepers lived in neither region, but along the borders. These men lived on the periphery, physically, socially, and religiously. Nobody wanted them as residents.

When Jesus was accosted by ten lepers, they cried out, "Jesus, Master, have mercy on us!" Luke would have us to know that of these ten lepers, one of them was a Samaritan. This is an important fact to consider, as there was deeply rooted enmity between the Jews and Samaritans. The Jews believed that Samaritans were morally inferior. Yet this small colony of lepers set aside their racial hatred and bonded together because of their common tragedy. They were driven to each other by a common misery.

We have some modern-day examples of the kind of misery and tragedy that bonds people from all walks of life together. The most significant example this nation has seen in a while happened on September 11, 2001, when the world watched as the most powerful nation in the world stood vulnerable in the face of the most vicious terrorist attack in history. On that day, the symbols of America's financial power—the Twin Towers of New York's World Trade Center—imploded, taking thousands of lives as they crumbled to the ground. As we watched the towering infernos with horror, meanwhile, America's symbol of military power—the Pentagon—suffered great damage at the hands of terrorists. Finally, the nation awaited anxiously as another airplane, some believe bound for America's symbol of political power—the White House—was diverted, eventually crashing in a Pennsylvania field. As the nation absorbed the horror of the day, Americans from coast to coast bonded in a spirit of patriotism. "We" had been attacked. Not white Americans, not black Americans, not brown, or red, or yellow Americans, but "we" had been attacked.

In the days following September 11, 2001, certain vivid images reminding us of the horror we had endured flashed across the television screen. On particularly poignant image was that of the survivors of the Twin Towers attacks walking away from the site. Everyone who was in the vicinity when the buildings crumbled was covered with ash. No matter what their race or ethnicity, everyone who walked away from the scene was the same color—ash. The camera panned a sea of ashen people moving perfunctorily away from the place that had been so familiar to them. People of all races and religions were helping each other as human beings in need. Comedian Richard Pryor has shared his personal experience with such tragedy, after a nearly fatal fire landed him in the burn unit of a Los Angeles-area hospital. Afterward, Pryor reflected on the experience with humor, noting that in the burn unit there is no racism, no black or white, because everybody is the same color—burned.

In these and similar circumstances, we find a great law of life— common misfortune breaks down artificial barriers. In their common tragedy, the ten lepers had forgotten that there was one Samaritan, an outsider, among them. They only saw themselves as men in need.

That bonds are formed at the hands of misfortune is also borne out in the animal kingdom. For example, I recall a documentary in which a deer and a wolf had huddled together on a high cliff. A rising flood caused these two natural enemies to come together in search of a common interest—safety. Similarly, common tragedy caused this interracial company of ten societal misfits to cry out with a loud, but unified voice, "Jesus, have mercy on us! Perhaps only their collective voice could get Jesus' attention. One of the symptoms of leprosy is a hoarse whisper. So, it may be reasoned that they needed each other's voices to amplify their plea. The lepers had to plan together and encourage each other so that their voices would be heard in unison. Their cooperation paid off—they got Jesus' attention.

When they got Jesus' attention, He gave them a bewildering command, "Go and show yourself to the priest." The priests were the medicine men of Jesus' day, as well as the community board of health. In order to reenter society, the lepers had to be certified by the priests as having been healed. It is interesting that Jesus told the lepers to go and show themselves to the priests before there was any sign of healing, which makes it seem like a form of cruel mockery. It would be like telling a single woman who desires marriage "Go and get your marriage license" before she even finds a husband. It is like telling a poor, inner city kid "Go enroll in college" before he gets his tuition. It is like telling a homeless person, "Go and rent a moving van," before he even has a home to go to. It is like telling an unemployed person, "Go and buy yourself a new wardrobe" before she even gets the job.

Jesus gave them no promise of healing nor did He offer them sympathy. Despite the fact that Jesus was not forthcoming with any blessings, faith realizes that one has to believe that certain things will happen before the blessing is actually possessed. Hebrews 11:1 substantiates this spiritual truth. So in obedience to the Master, all ten lepers went to the priest. The text says that as they went, they were healed. Every step they took was a step of healing. The more they walked toward the priests the more health and vitality crept into their bodies. As they went in obedience to the Lord they acted on His command.

It's almost like they were being blessed and didn't even know it. Many of the blessings God's gives us are never revealed to us as such.

For instance, people gain healing as they get on with life, as they heal from a divorce or other major loss, as they move beyond the victimization of child abuse, and as they generally move forward and get over the past. As much as we would like for them to be, life conversions are not always instantaneous and Pauline. Many, if not most of our conversion experiences are gradual revelations that come to us as we take steps in obedience.

Healing came to the ten lepers as they made their way to the priests in obedience to the Master. The lepers had been living on the borders, but they moved toward something significant as they went. A lot of people are not healed because they are stuck along the borders and refuse to move beyond toward healing. They keep nursing, rehearsing, and cursing the same wounds. But in prayer we disperse them and, God will reverse them. God never blesses us while we are idle, but while we are working, exercising active faith.

These ten lepers had much in common. All of them were lepers. They all were ostracized from religious and community life. They all cried out to Jesus for deliverance. And they all obeyed Jesus' command to show themselves to the priest. As they went all of them experienced restored health. But while they had so much in common, there was one critical attitude that separated one of the lepers from his nine colleagues. The leper who stood apart from the rest was the Samaritan. Like the others, he prayed a "Give me" prayer. But unlike the other nine lepers he came back to Jesus with a "thank You" prayer. He got on his knees and worshiped God with thanksgiving. And with sadness in His voice, Jesus asked, "Were there not ten healed? Where are the nine?"

I believe this text helps us to understand the percentage of "Give me" prayers versus "Thank You" prayers. If the ten lepers are an indication, then only 10 percent of the prayers rendered to God are offered for the sole purpose of saying "Thank You." The other nine lepers had become so absorbed in the gift that they forgot the Giver. Only one of them came back and said "Thank You" for the healing that so significantly impacted their lives. Jesus said to the Samaritan, "Arise, your faith has made you whole."

What does that mean? It is not implying that the other nine's healing would be cancelled because of their ingratitude. God does not withdraw God's gifts just because we don't say, "Thank You." What it does mean, however—in the words of author Bruce Larsen—is *There's a Lot More to Health than Not Being Sick* (W Publishing Group, 1984). Just because they were physically healthy does not mean that they still were not. Had the nine come back to thank Jesus, it would have indicated that they also had gained spiritual healthy and wholeness as they went. A lot of people have physical health, but they are still sick—egotistical, self-centered, petty, jealous, and spiritually unfocused. Wholeness comes only when we experience gratitude for what we have received. That means moving beyond mere entitlements.

This principle that tangible benefits were gained by persons in the Bible *As They Went* in obedience to the Lord simply means that believers experience unimaginable blessings as we act in accordance with God's will. Those of us whose hope is in the Lord don't live on explanations; we live by faith. And this principle is not only true for the ten lepers, but it is a principle modeled by many of our Bible heroes. As Esther went, she experienced a sense of calling and empowerment to aid her people. As Naomi went, she experienced the providence of God, who made a way for two women who had nothing but love for each other and faith in the Lord. It's easy for believers to get caught up in the paralysis of analysis. But our response to God should always be like that of Abraham, who went to where the Lord was calling him, even though he had no idea where he was going. As he went, he moved closer to the fulfillment of God's promise to him.

In the spiritual journey of life, we choose whether we will walk in the direction of obedience or away from Him into spiritual abyss. As Saul went, he moved away from obedience and was totally unaware that the Lord was no longer with him. As Samson went, he moved farther and farther away from the Lord, all the while not aware that the Lord had left Him. The lost recounted in Matthew 25 were totally unaware that they were ignoring Jesus. *As They Went...* they missed opportunities to serve the Lord. Their experiences, whether they move closer or farther away from the Lord *As They Went,* reveal to us that as we go through life often we are not even aware that we are changing. But in our forties, we look back at the way we were in our twenties and thirties, and we realize how far the Lord has brought us. In our sixties, we look back over our forties and fifties and thank the Lord that we've come so far. If we walk in obedience to the Lord, we come closer to Him with every step. Every step we take is important because each step is a decision whether to move closer to or farther away from the Lord. As we go we plant a thought and we reap an attitude; we plant an attitude and we reap a behavior; we plant a behavior and we reap a character; we plant a character and we reap a destiny.

In *As They Went...*, we embark upon an enlightening journey with noteworthy Bible personalities such as Enoch, Abraham, Joshua, Peter, Philip, and many others. Through these powerful and inspiring stories, this book explores how God's people have experienced God's blessings simply *As They Went....* And just as they did, we too will experience His blessings as we go where He leads.

Enoch walked with God;
then he was no more,
because God took him away.

Intimacy

Genesis 5:24

There are four simple words, "he walked with God" that reveal the blessing gain by Enoch as he went. Enoch experienced intimacy with God as he journeyed through life—so much so that he was simply taken up to heaven.

The fifth chapter of Genesis reads like an obituary in the local newspaper. There is a refrain: "and he died." Adam lived and he died. Adam's son Seth lived and he died. And so it is recorded for Enoch, Kenan, Mahalalel, Jared, and so on. In fact, the entire Book of Genesis is the fulfillment of a promise made to Adam and Eve. God promised them that the day that they ate from the tree of knowledge of good and evil would signal certain death.

With Adam and Eve's disobedience, the cycle of life and death began and is recorded in Genesis. Aside from the number of years they lived, there is nothing eventful or noteworthy about the names entered in chapter five, except for that of one man. When the life of Enoch is reported, there is a variance from the simple record of life and death. He is like a gardenia growing in the desert. While everyone else died, God took Enoch, and he went on to heaven without enduring the transitional phase of death.

Enoch has a significant role in the Jewish faith, though little space is given to him in the Old Testament. While Christians believe that Jesus is the promised Messiah, the Jews believe that He is yet to come. They contend that the Messiah cannot appear until two people return—one is Elijah, who also bypassed death and was taken up to heaven in a fiery chariot (2 Kings. 2:11). Another is Enoch.

Many people are not familiar with Enoch because he does not have an extensive listing in the Bible. His name is not synonymous with a biblical event, like Noah and the ark, or Daniel and the lion's den. Enoch is not as well known as more prominent biblical personalities, but when the eleventh chapter of Hebrews was compiled and the great hall of faith was pulled together, one of the names that is listed among the great patriarchs and matriarchs of our faith is Enoch.

Why was he entered in the hall of faith? Enoch's testimony to the Judeo-Christian world can be summarized in four short, yet powerful words—he walked with God. That is all that the Bible really tells us about Enoch. He did not rescue a nation, like Moses did. He did not give birth to a Savior, like Mary did. He did not wrestle with God, like Jacob did. He did not defeat a giant, like David did. He did not lead an army, like Deborah did. All that we know about Enoch is that he walked with God. What a reputation to have! Any time someone from his village wanted to find him and asked, "Where is Enoch?" the response must have been, "I don't know, the last time I saw him he was walking with God."

Most of us probably would not have selected Enoch to be a member of the hall of faith found in Hebrews 11. He didn't do anything that most of us would consider noteworthy. But the Bible says that God was pleased with Enoch because he walked with Him. Nothing pleases God so much as when we are in close communion and fellowship with Him. The word walk is nothing more than a euphemism for intimacy with God. A person who walks with God does not leave Him in the sanctuary after service is over on Sunday. Rather, a person who walks intimately with the Lord will take the name of Jesus everywhere.

If you think about it, there probably are not many Christians you would describe as having an intimate fellowship with the Lord. That may be due partly to the fact that the church does not stress the need for believers to walk closely with the Lord. Usually preachers focus on the "work" of a Christian. Thank God for the work. We need laborers in the vineyard. God does not call anyone to be a pew potato. God's work must be done by our hands. He did not save us to sit, but to serve and to live a life of usefulness. He has something for every one of us to do. That is why when we get to heaven we will wait to hear Him say to us, "Well done, good and faithful servant" (Matthew 25:23). He will not say, "well thought…" or "well intended…" The phrase "well done" implies that work was initiated and completed. When there is a separation of the sheep and the goats, it will not be a random sorting. Jesus has already established the criteria. To the sheep He will say, "I was hungry, and you worked and got me fed. I was naked, but you didn't hold a humanities hearing on the appropriate-ness of my appearance. You worked and clothed me. I was in jail, and you came and visited me. When I was homeless, you didn't chastise me for being lazy or attempt to pacify me with platitudes like, 'I'm praying for you.' You made room for me and took me in. And because of the work you have done I say to you, 'Come. You are blessed for having done the work of My Father. Come inherit the heaven that has been prepared for you.'" Kingdom work is important.

But as important as work is, it does not supercede the importance of walking with the Lord. When Jesus went to Bethany and visited His friends, Martha went to work preparing the meal (Luke 10:38-42). Meanwhile, her sister Mary sat at Jesus' feet, listening to His teaching. Martha got upset and wanted Jesus to tell Mary to come into the kitchen. But Jesus told her, "Mary has chosen the better thing." Jesus acknowledged Martha's work, but He affirmed Mary's walk. Working in the church is a good thing to do, but walking in intimacy with the Lord is the better thing.

God saves us primarily because He loves us and wants us to spend eternity with Him in heaven. He also saves us so that we can work with and for Him. The great church reformer Martin Luther observed, "We are not saved by faith and works. We are saved by faith that works." Though the work is critical, it is not the primary reason we are saved. God was getting things done before He saved us! For centuries, God struggled to have intimacy with Israel. He loves His creation and wants us to love Him so much that we gladly work for Him.

If we walk in intimacy with the Lord, the Kingdom work will get done; but the reverse does not hold true. It is possible to work for the Lord and not know the Lord. Albert Einstein's wife once was asked if she knew her husband's theory of relativity. She said, "No, I don't know his theory, but I know him." Some Christians are the opposite. They memorize scriptures, they know what they've heard about Him in sermons and songs, but they don't know Him. There are even preachers who are in total disharmony with the Lord. There are choir members who do not know the Lord they sing about. There are deacons who are totally ignorant of Jesus' servanthood.

The fact that God and Enoch walked together for so long indicates kindred spirits or like-mindedness. God knows each of us, and He wants us to know Him as Enoch knew Him. More than anything, the Lord wants us to have true intimacy with Him, not some kind of formal relationship that is acceptable in the eyes of society. He wants to be more than just a spiritual one-night stand. An intimate relationship with God can be understood in the context of a close covenantal relationship, like marriage. To have a good relationship, a husband and wife need to spend time together. They have to communicate with each other. They have to walk together along life's journey. They need shared values and mutual goals. To have an enduring relationship, a couple needs to be going in the same direction, even if it is the wrong one! Two crackheads probably could maintain a relationship with one another because their association is based on a certain understanding. But if one spouse hits the pipe while the other spouse is a sanctified, Holy Ghost-filled Christian, more than likely they will not make a fruitful union.

A good indicator of a person being in love is that the person always wants to spend time with his or her beloved. Conversely, a clear sign that a relationship has begun to disintegrate is when the two parties no longer desire to associate with one another. The same thing happens in our relationship with God. He wants us to have a loving, intimate relationship with Him. When we have that kind of relationship with Him, nothing makes us happier than being in communion with the Lord. But if our relationship with God has deteriorated, we spend little time with Him. We don't seek His face. We don't find joy in communicating with Him. We no longer try to show our love for Him. Our prayers are perfunctory and stale. We go to church because we are afraid of what may happen if we don't. Everything else takes precedence over spending time with God. All these things are signs of spiritual decline and a deteriorating relationship with the Lord.

It is painful to be in a failing relationship. It is agonizing to watch a relationship deteriorate. It is distressing to see a once-faithful Christian fall away from the fold. It is painful to God when one of His beloved turns from Him. More than anything, God wants us to walk with Him. I imagine that God daily asks, "Can we just talk a little bit? Do you have a little time when you can just turn off your television and your cellular phone and your pager so that we can spend time together?" Some of us can't spend enough time with God because our pager won't stop beeping, and we think we have to return the call right away. If our cellular phone won't stop ringing we think we can't just turn it off for a while. Our favorite television show can't wait, or we can't turn down the car radio.

God does not want to compete with our electronic devices. He wants to spend time with us without worldly distractions.

An important part of our relationship with God is attitude. We must remember that when we go to church we are not doing God a favor. While many of us go to church regularly, we treat worship as though it is giving God His due, ignoring Him for the remainder of the week. Many of us go to church on Sunday and "get our praise on," but don't show Him our love during the week. We don't tell Him that we love Him. We don't tell Him how much He means to us. We don't thank Him for our job, for waking us up, for bringing us through hard times. God wants to be intimate with us and these are the things people do to and for one another when they are intimately involved with each other.

What pleased God about Enoch was that each day he walked with God. Enoch did more than live and die; he walked with the Lord. He intentionally maintained an intimate relationship with the Lord. But so many people are not capable of having the kind of relationship with God that Enoch did. They can't do it because it is impossible to walk with God unless we are willing to go in the direction that God leads us. He is not going to walk with us in sin. There are some places we can't take God. We can't take God to Motel 6® if we are going there to sin. We can't take God with us into the crack house or the strip club. We should not go any place or be with anyone that God cannot accompany us.

Many doors must have been shut in Enoch's face because he couldn't take God with him there. He probably didn't have a lot of friends because he couldn't take God with him in their company. When we walk in the same direction as God, we have to go where He goes. We can't walk with everybody—like people who don't share either our faith or our nature. A lot of us know people we walked with before we began walking with God; but that had to stop when we realized that they would take us in a direction that was opposite from God's. Some Christians are messed up today because they have been walking with folks who are not walking with the Lord. It is important for God's people to understand that some people have natures that are contrary to that of Christ. We have to be careful about whom we walk with and whom we allow to walk with us. It is possible to get cancer from second-hand smoke. A person can get a "contact high" simply by being in close proximity to someone smoking marijuana. In the same way, Christians can be adversely affected by associating with those engaging in acts that are contrary to God. But if we walk with God, we never have to worry about going in the wrong direction.

Psalm 1 says blessed is the one who does not walk in the counsel of the ungodly, or stand in the way of sinners, or sit in the seat with scorners. Notice the intimacy that develops in this psalm. We start out walking, then we end up standing; finally we sit, because after constant association, we become more comfortable in His presence.

When God walks with us, there are benefits. We need intimacy with the Lord because there are some problems we can't solve, some mountains we can't climb, some rivers we can't cross, and some sicknesses we can't endure unless the Lord is with us. No matter who we are or what we acquire, all of us face times when no one and nothing but Jesus can see us through.

Money, power, influence, and education are good to have but they are no substitute for intimacy with God. Enoch did not make all the money in the world; he couldn't walk with God and spend all of his time worrying about his investments. It's better to have a lot of Jesus and a little money than to have all the money, all the friends, or all the opportunities this world has to offer and little or no Jesus. Sooner or later, we realize that true joy and contentment cannot be purchased at the mall. They come as the result of intimacy with the Lord.

We do not need anybody's permission to walk in intimacy with the Lord. Wherever we go, He is with us. When life becomes difficult and problems overwhelm, when we sense there is a need for maturity and growth, when our patience runs thin, or we are grieving because of loss of hope and unfulfilled dreams, we can hear God saying, "Let's go for a walk..."

What Enoch did to earn his place in the hall of faith was simple...but certainly not easy. Walking with God day by day is not easy. Sometimes we want to give back to the world what it has given to us. Sometimes we are tempted to win by cheating. Sometimes doing the worldly, human thing seems much less complicated than asking, "What would Jesus do?" Intimacy with God does not mean perfection, rather it means walking in God's direction. Along our Christian journey we may stumble or fall, but because of our intimate association with God, we will not stay down, and we certainly will not be defeated. This sentiment is beautifully and poetically expressed in the hymn "Leaning on the Everlasting Arms," which is really about one's relationship with God. The arms of other human beings and false idols cannot uphold us. Only the everlasting arms of God can sustain us through life's trials.

The Motive of Intimacy with God

As we mirror our own spiritual walk with that of Enoch's there are a couple of important factors to consider. First, Enoch didn't begin walking with God until after his first child was born. That means he was a man of some maturity. He had lived and experienced some things. He knew how to lean on the everlasting arms. He knew that the best life is one spent in close communion with the Lord.

Second, Enoch lived in the Antediluvian age. There was an awesome responsibility in that age. With each generation, the world was steadily growing more wicked. By the time of Noah, the world was filled with debauchery and sin. Enoch may have known that the Flood or some similar catastrophic event was coming, so he asked God to, "Walk with me."

Sometimes we are so deluged with problems to the extent that all we can do is plead, "God, walk with me." And He will. But when we petition Him, we must be willing to go where He leads us, through the pathways that He directs us—and initially, that may not be where we want to go. Some people say, "God, walk with me." And what they really mean is, "Lord, follow me. I want you to go where I want to take you." But to walk with the Lord is to trust Him. This depth of intimacy occurs by faith, not by sight. Faith is what enables us to continue on the walk. On our own, we don't have the power to walk with God. Our strength to walk is maintained through our faith in God.

Far too often, the request for God to "walk with me" may be made to God only after all other efforts and resources are exhausted. Many of us are motivated to walk with God only after we are faced with decisions and problems that we cannot manage alone.

The Mystery of Intimacy with God

Enoch overcame death because God took him. At the close of a day of walking with God, the Lord must have said, "Enoch, you're closer to My house than you are to yours. Why don't you go home with Me?" Enoch went through the first, second and third heavens. He saw the first heaven by day, the second heaven by night, and the third heaven by faith. God's Word does not tell us about Enoch's work. The Bible only records the work of His servants as a means of revealing their walk.

What is your greatest achievement as a believer? Is it your work, or is it your walk? The only thing that will last will be your walk. People may remember some of your work, but they will not forget your walk. They may remember the work that you do because you have walked with the Lord. But the lasting impression is always the walk. Your living example of intimacy with God will not be forgotten.

Then God said, "Yes, but your wife Sarah will bear you a son, and you will call him Isaac. I will establish my covenant with him as an everlasting covenant for his descendants after him."

Genesis 17:19, NIV

Providence

Genesis 17:19

Abraham endured many trials and tribulations, but through it all his strength lay in the promise of God. As Abraham went on His life journey in faith, he experienced the providence of God.

In this passage, God told Abraham, "Your wife Sarah will bear you a son and you will call his name Isaac. I will establish my covenant with him, an everlasting covenant for his descendants after him. I will establish my covenant with Isaac, your son, and it shall be an everlasting covenant."

As always, God fulfilled His promise to Abraham and Sarah. Yet in chapter 22, God seems to contradict this promise. A few years after the birth of Isaac God tested Abraham. God said, Abraham, take your only son Isaac, whom you love, and go to the region of Moriah and sacrifice him as a burnt offering on one of the mountains I shall tell you about." Early the next morning, Abraham got up and saddled his donkey. With him were two servants and his son Isaac. When Abraham had cut enough wood for the burnt offering he set off for the place God had told him about. On the third day, Abraham looked up and saw the place in the distance.

God will test the authenticity of our faith. He will send us through a test to determine our level of spiritual maturity. Conversely, the devil tempts us in order to defeat us. But God tests us to develop us. Since God tests us for our edification, any test that believers experience is for our spiritual development and maturation. And as we are faithful to the test we experience God's providence. First Peter 1:6-7 reads, "In this time you greatly rejoice, though now, for a little while, you may have suffered grief through all kinds of trials." Verse 7 tells us why God lets us have trials. He says that these have come so that our faith may be proved genuine and may result in praise, glory and honor when Jesus Christ is revealed.

Along the journey of our faith development, our spiritual maturity level increases as a direct result of divine testing. We don't always know it when we are in the midst of being tested by God, but when we look back on it, we can recognize that the test helped to develop us and not to diminish us. God tests us because a faith that cannot be tested cannot be trusted. Before God uses us, before He demonstrates divine providence, He tests to show what we can do. God already knows what we can do, but He wants us to know what we can do. He wants to be sure that we are ready before He sends us out for further service.

In the business world, certain products don't go on the market until they first undergo certain tests. Certain medicines are not allowed to go on the market until the Food and Drug Administration is satisfied that they have passed certain tests. New automobiles are not put on the road until they go through certain tests. And believers generally do not experience great demonstrations of God's providence until they first pass some tests. These tests are ongoing. We never get too old to be tested. We will never be so saved or reach some stratosphere of spirituality that we will rise above spiritual testing.

Sometimes our test may be job related. The test might come though our relationships. It could be a financial test or a family test. No matter how hard it may seem, it's just a test. When the

Emergency Broadcasting System issues a test on a television station that we're watching, we don't panic when we hear the signal noise. We don't call the cable company or kick the television. We wait for the 60-second test to be completed and resume watching the show, knowing that if there is a national emergency the system will operate as it should.

God tested Abraham because Abraham had a reputation as being a man of faith. When God called Abraham for the time of testing, he responded, "Here I am." Abraham was not trying to help God locate him geographically; rather he was indicating his spiritual location. Abraham's response says much about his spiritual address. I can imagine God asking, "Where do you live, Abraham?" And Abraham responded, "I live on Here-I-Am Street. Wherever you want me to go, whatever you want me to do, that's where I live."

When God called Abraham for the time of testing, he responded, "Here I am."

All of God's people should know their spiritual address. Some of us are lost simply because we don't know our address. The spiritually lost avoid God or ignore Him altogether. God is not concerned with where our house is, and He's not concerned about our zip code. He wants to know our spiritual address. And when He asks, we ought to be able to say, "God, my spiritual address is 'Here I am.'"

God told Abraham, "Take your only son, whom you love, to one of the mountains I will show you and offer him as a burnt offering." Now Abraham had another son named Ishmael, but God told Abraham, "I'm going to bless you through Isaac." But since God said it and

Abraham believed him Ishmael was dismissed, which means that Abraham did not make any contingency plans in the event that God didn't come through for him and spare Isaac.

That's what faith does. Faith says that if God tells me to do something that I make no contingencies in case God's going to fail. God is not going to fail. God is going to do what He says He will to do. He will provide for His people. Many of us trust God, but we got some contingencies just in case. People develop contingencies because they are not yet ready to trust in the providence of God.

God says, "I want you to trust Me," but in the event that God doesn't come through for us, then we keep certain phone numbers. We maintain certain unhealthy relationships just in case God doesn't come through for us. We try to find a way to make it happen just in case God reneges. If God says "I want you to leave that liquor alone," yet the person makes an effort to stay on good terms with the liquor man, the drug man, or the candy man, that is not a statement of faith and trust in God's providence. God says, "I want you quit your job and go to school to prepare for full time ministry," but the one who is called still tries to find alternatives. That is not an example of trust in the Lord.

A person easily can say, "I'm gonna trust the Lord. The Lord don't want me sleeping around, so I'm going to stop." But then the person doesn't get rid of that little black book of temptation. Instead, the person keeps a contingency plan, just in case. By contrast, faith steps out there and says, "I'm gonna put all my trust in God. And I don't need a contingency plan because God is true to His Word."

God tested Abraham by telling him, "I want you to take your son, your only son whom you love, and offer him as a sacrifice." Abraham truly loved Isaac, not just because the lad was his own flesh and blood, but because Isaac represented Abraham's past. It was because of Isaac that Abraham had left culture, family, friends, and homeland—all because God promised to give him a son. Abraham was 75 and his wife Sarah was 65 and childless, but he left everything and went wandering in the wilderness with no forwarding address. He didn't have a forwarding address because he didn't know where he was going to end up. Abraham trusted God and God honored his faithfulness; therefore Isaac represented Abraham's past.

Isaac also represented Abraham's present. The name Isaac literally means "laughter" because the circumstances under which Abraham and Sarah became parents was laughable. Sarah laughed at the thought of becoming a mother at age 90, married to a man who was nearly 100. Any 90-year-old woman would laugh if she were married to a 99-year-old man. Long before the invention of Viagra®, Sarah could not conceive that such a marvelous thing could happen to them at such an old age. Isaac kept Abraham laughing. He gave Abraham a reason to get up in the morning. People don't stop laughing just because they grow old; they can grow old because they stop laughing. Abraham and Sarah were laughing despite the fact that He would have to dip into his pension to buy Pampers® and infant formula. Abraham had joy, something to look forward to, because he had Isaac. His son was his pride and his joy. Isaac was his past, Isaac was his present, but Isaac also was his future. Chapter 17 reveals that God said through Isaac that He would bless Abraham's descendants.

But God told Abraham to take his past, his present, and his future and destroy it by making his son a burnt offering. That meant there would be nothing salvageable because a burnt offering means cremation. As he listened to God, Abraham must have wondered, "What kind of absurd request is this?" But it was a test. Despite his confusion, and perhaps even fear, early the next morning

Abraham got up, saddled his donkey, and took two of his servants and his beloved son to the place where God would lead him. After he had cut enough wood for the burnt offering, Abraham set out for the place God told him about. After three days of traveling, Abraham looked up and saw the place in the distance.

Since Abraham got up early the next morning, that likely meant he had a restless night. Strange things can happen at night. It was at night when Abraham heard the call to take his beloved Isaac and offer him as a burnt offering. But the fact that he got up early the next morning means that he obeyed God with promptness. He didn't wait a week or even a single day, unlike many of us when God calls us to do something. One thing that characterizes personal faith is that when God tells us to do something, we do it immediately. We do not procrastinate. We don't need God to explain anything. God says, "You do it," and it's done. Whatever God has instructed us to do, we should do it with promptness.

Not only was Abraham prompt, he was prepared. He cut some wood, got some servants, fire-making tools, and a knife in order to do what God told him. And we can always tell if our intent is to obey God because whenever we're going to obey God, we always prepare ourselves for obedience. That is true even when it comes to our worship today. When we really want to worship, we prepare by getting ourselves ready.

When I was a boy, my parents made us get ready for church. We had to get our shoes ready, we had to have our church clothes ready on Saturday. We didn't come

One thing that characterizes personal faith is that when God tells us to do something, we do it immediately.

to church fumbling and stumbling, looking for our offering money, our Bible, or straightening out our clothes. Any time we take God seriously, we get ready. When we trust in the providence of God, by faith our actions lead us to "act as if." A person whom God has called to preach will get ready to preach, even if there is no pulpit in which to preach. The called one prepares by going to school and learning to do what God has for him or her to do. If God says to someone, "I'm gonna give you a house," that person should already have begin to prepare financially for what God is about to give.

My understanding of success is when preparation meets opportunity. And many times God has given us the opportunity, but we have not prepared ourselves. That's why I like what Bishop T. D. Jakes says: "Get ready! Get ready! Get ready!" When St. Stephen Baptist Church began acquiring additional property, it was not all purchased overnight. It took 22 years to accumulate the land on which our present worship facility sits. I didn't know why we were buying the land way back between 1979 and 1981. But in His divine omniscience, God knew far in advance that we were going to need more space for the various ministries we now have. All we had to do was to faithfully keep doing what God told us to do. He had prepared the way. Now St. Stephen has an appointment with destiny because our faithfulness has intersected with God's providence, and that's what happens when God's people are faithful, we intersect with God's providence.

Abraham was prompt, Abraham was prepared, but Abraham also was persistent. He kept walking on a 70-mile course that took three days. That means he walked about 23 miles a day. That's a lot of walking, especially when you're on your way to do something that will break your heart. But no matter what he may have been feeling, Abraham kept on treading toward Mount Moriah.

What is it that can keep believers on the journey of faith when we have to walk toward a mountain that we really don't want to climb? Whether we are facing debilitating sickness, unemployment, financial troubles, or troubled relationships, at times in our lives we all face mountains we don't want to climb. But what keeps us going down a path that we have been called to walk but don't want to?

Surely Abraham did not want to walk from Beer-sheba to Mount Moriah. What kept Abraham going? The same thing that will keep all of God's people going—faith in God's promise. God had promised back in Genesis 17 to bless Abraham with a son, and through his son Isaac all his descendants would be blessed. So armed with that promise Abraham told his servants, "Stay here. I'm going up the mountain, but I'm not coming back by myself. We both will come back because God made a promise. I don't know how we're going to come back. I don't know how God's going to work it out. I don't know how God's going to fix it. Maybe after I burn up Isaac and all the ashes are in the air, maybe God's going to gather all the ashes and form the dust from those ashes and blow into Isaac like he blew into the first man. I don't know how God's going to work this thing out, I just know that he will and we will return." Now that's faith! Abraham explained to his servants that he and his son were going to worship the Lord, and that they both would be back. He knew that through his faithful act of obedience and worship, somehow he would come back down that mountain with his precious son.

Faith says "I don't know how I'm gonna pay my bills, but they're going to be paid. I don't know how I'm going to make it, but I'm going to make it. I don't know how I'm going to deal with all these pressures that I'm under, but I'm gonna make. I don't know how tomorrow is going to turn out, but I believe I'm going to make it. And I believe I'm going to make it because God is going to keep His promise."

God promises to be our Shepherd. He promises to provide for, care for, and watch over His people in a way that we cannot do for ourselves. God says that we shall not want. He promises to prepare a table before us in the presence of our enemies. We can never know how God will work it out, all we have to do is just believe that God will do it. God's Word tells us that all things work together for good of those who love the Lord. So we don't ever know how God's going to work it out, but we can trust that God will.

Every child of God has been there at one time or another, when all of options seem gone and all doors seem shut. Everything looks bleak and dark, yet God's people stand confidently, believing that somehow God is going to work it out. We trust in this because of God's track record. God has already worked it out. God opens doors. God raises up friends. God puts people in strategic places during our times of need. We don't know where these angels of divine providence came from, but they were there when we needed them. As my Mama used to say, "All night and all day, angels watching over me, my Lord."

When God sends us to our own Mount Moriah, we must go there will the full confidence that we will meet His providence at the mountaintop. Abraham climbed Mount Moriah, going up there to offer up laughter; to offer up his past, present and future. He got to the top of the mountain, took the wood, and built an altar. As he built the altar and tied up his beloved son, Isaac looked at his father and said, "Daddy, I see the wood. I see the altar. I see your knife, but where is the lamb

Everything looks bleak and dark, yet God's people stand confidently, believing that somehow God is going to work it out.

for the sacrifice?" Abraham simply replied, "Son, the Lord will provide."

We know God has many names—Jehovah Raah, meaning "the Lord is my shepherd;" Jehovah Tsidkenu, "the Lord is my righteousness;" and Jehovah Nissi, "the Lord is my banner." One of God's names for God is Jehovah Jireh, which means, "the Lord will provide." And God will provide. The Lord will provide whatever we need—food, shelter, rest, peace, friends, deliverance—anything that we need. Come what may, God will take care of His people. When my mother was alive, she had a group that sang, "Who opened doors that I cannot see? Jesus will. Yes, He will. He'll fight my battles if I keep still. He will. Yes, He will. Don't understand how, but He will, and right then."

Come what may, God will take care of His people.

As Abraham was about to plunge a dagger into his son, God spoke up again and said "Abraham, do your son no harm." Abraham had passed his test. As Abraham looked up, there strapped in a thicket was a ram. God provided the sacrifice. Because of Abraham's faith, he saw the Lord's providence. His blessing was awaiting him in the thicket. Abraham didn't have to chase or trap the ram. The Lord had provided! While Abraham was climbing one side of the mountain, God had a ram climbing up the other side. With our limited vision and insight, we have no way of knowing what's going on the other side of the mountain we're climbing. All we can see is our own side. But on the other side, God has a ram caught in the bush and so that it can't get away until it's time for His designated servant to get it.

When we lose our job on one side of the mountain, God is sending a new company to town on the other side. When we're broke on this side of the mountain, God is sending new resources up the other side. When friends walk out on us on this side of the mountain, God is sending new friends on the other side. When we're crying on this side of the mountain, God is sending joy on the other side of the mountain.

Because of His proven track record of providence, we must trust in the Lord with all our heart and lean not to our own understanding and in all ways acknowledge God and God will direct our path. God is a provider and a promise keeper. God always will do just what God has said He will do. Even when our back is against the wall, God makes a way out of no way. As our forebears sang, "Jesus, be a fence, all around me." And when God comes through and makes a way for us, we shouldn't be ashamed so shout, "Hallelujah! Thank You!"

*And on that very day
the LORD brought
the Israelites out of Egypt
by their divisions.*

Exodus 12:51, NIV

EMPOWERMENT

Exodus 7—11

Moses did not start off as a powerful leader. When God met him at the burning bush, Moses was a fugitive from justice. He had low self-esteem, and was not particularly strong in his speech. But as he went on his faith journey in the Lord, he gained empowerment to deliver a nation and, in turn, empower an entire nation.

L et my people go!" is a declarative sentence that is both familiar and empowering to the African American faith community. These words of Moses, these four simple yet powerful words, have been the anthem of oppressed people throughout the ages. People who have struggled for liberation and who have struggled against oppression have found inspiration in God's words that Moses delivered to Pharaoh, "Let my people go!"

This simple, but powerful sentence was chanted as blacks in South Africa fought to dismantle apartheid and sweep it into the dustpan of history. These four words were the inspiration behind the freedom struggle in Birmingham as Martin Luther King Jr. and other freedom fighters went into nonviolent warfare against Bull Connor and armed with his vicious police dogs and mighty fire hoses that were so strong they could tear the bark off trees.

Not only are these words inspirational to those who seek freedom from systemic oppression, but also to those who seek freedom from enslavement in their personal lives. Oppression is not only systemic and structural, it is also personal. Many of us are enslaved by the pharaohs of poor eating habits, the pharaohs of nicotine, the pharaohs of alcohol and drug addiction, the pharaohs of a demented past, or the pharaohs of trying to live up to other people's expectations. Whatever our pharaoh is, whether personal or systemic, we all can find inspiration in Moses' powerfully authoritative command, "Let my people go!" Even though it took Egyptian Pharaoh Ramses a while to figure it out, these four powerful words remind us that no one and nothing has a right to hold us bound. They remind us that we all have a right to be free and self-determined.

Moses made a demand, standing on the full power and authority of the Almighty,

Beyond their capacity to inspire, the command "Let my people go!" has the capacity to instruct, because it reminds us that people who want to be free cannot simply make a request for it to happen. Freedom is a right that must be demanded. Moses did not ask the ruler of Egypt, "Pharaoh, will you consider letting God's people go?" Nor did Moses say, "Will you give prayerful consideration to letting God's people go?" Moses made a demand, standing on the full power and authority of the Almighty, "Pharaoh, the God of Israel has said, 'Let my people go.'"

Moses issues a demand for liberation, not a suggestion. The reason why liberation must be demanded is because when a person desires to be free, whatever has that person bound is equally determined to stay in control. Whatever has someone bound will do everything in its power to keep that person bound. The oppressor will attempt to match and overpower the captive's determination to be free with an equal determination to maintain domination.

Consider Pharaoh's response to Moses. Pharaoh responded to Moses' demand with, "Who is this God you're talking about? I don't know Him, who is He? Well, Moses, you're talking to god, because in Egypt I am all that is divine. In fact, Moses, to prove to you that I'm divine, not only will I defy the demands of this invisible God, but also I will increase the workload of His people. They've been making bricks with government-supplied straw, but from this point on they have to find their own straw. And I still want the same quota of bricks at the end of the day. You got that, Moses? Go tell that to your God!"

Pharaoh defied God. He was obstinate, but he had every reason to be at the time of his encounter with Moses. The authority of the pharaoh of ancient Egypt was sovereign. So powerful was the ruler of Egypt that all truth was defined by what the pharaoh declared. That means if the pharaoh said that the sun was not shining, that became the people's reality. Whether the sun actually was shining or not was irrelevant. Even if the sun was shining that day, the people could not acknowledge it because pharaoh had said that it was not.

The Egyptians believed that pharaoh was a god and, moreover, central to the nation's relationship to the cosmic gods of the universe. The ruling pharaoh was believed to be the son of Ra, the sun god, and the incarnation of the god Horus. They believed that the pharaohs came to them from the gods, with the divine responsibility to rule the land. Pharaoh's word was law. He owned everything. Therefore, Egypt had no law codes, because the pharaoh alone sustained order and justice and insured

So powerful was the ruler of Egypt that all truth was defined by what the pharaoh declared.

the stability of society. Because the Egyptians believed that their fate was dependent on that of their pharaoh, seldom were there attempts to depose him and overthrow the government. So given pharaoh's understanding of his unquestioned authority, Moses' demand seemed all the more preposterous.

To give Moses a demonstration of his sovereignty in Egypt, Ramses increased Israel's suffering. Israel bore the burden, but the struggle was really a conflict between Pharaoh and God. Israel got caught in the middle of spiritual warfare. This makes me believe that sometimes when we catch hell, it isn't personal. The devil is not really after us, it's God he's trying to get. But because the devil has figured out that his arms are too short to box with God, the only option at his disposal is to get at the heart of God—His people. For example, if a person wanted to get me but could not get to me, the worst thing that person could do to me is to harm one of my children or my wife. To hurt my children or my wife is to hurt me. The devil knows he can't get God because God is so high no one can get over Him, and He's so low no one can go under Him. God is so wide no one can go around Him, and so deep no one can penetrate Him. So the devil says, "I am going to hurt the children of God." It's nothing personal, it's just the devil. But isn't that a foolish thing for Satan to do? To think that he can fight God after all these centuries, isn't that asinine? To think that we can box with God is ridiculous. No one goes bear hunting with a switch.

The apostle Paul said, "For we wrestle not against flesh and blood, but against principalities, against powers,

To think that we can box with God is ridiculous. No one goes bear hunting with a switch.

against the rulers of the darkness of this world, against spiritual wickedness in high places." He further admonishes us to put on the whole armor of God so that we may be able to stand—not against our co-workers, not against the boss, but against the wiles of the devil. Given such a strong advisement, it is surprising that some people still do not believe in the devil. That's one of his best tricks; if we don't believe in him, we won't take the necessary precautions to defeat him. That means we might curse somebody out when we ought to be on our knees engaging in spiritual warfare. Not even Satan, whether we believe in him or not, can hinder the work of the Lord. Suppose a person doesn't like winter and stands outside in a bathing suit in mid-December and says, "Stop, winter." That will not stop the cold and snow. In the same manner, no one can stop God's will. No one can hinder King Jesus.

God responded to Pharaoh's abstinence by saying, "Well, Ramses, since you say you don't know who I am, allow me to introduce myself. I'm going to leave my calling card in the water. Through Egypt, the cradle of civilization runs the Nile River, which originates in Uganda and makes its way down to the Nile Valley. One day when Pharaoh went to take a drink, God turned the water in the Nile to blood. Then God said, "You still don't know me?" And suddenly frogs jumped from the river and landed everywhere. God then left another calling card—gnats all over the place. Again and again God introduced Himself to Ramses with plagues of darkness that covered the land, sores that infected the people and the livestock, locusts that destroyed all of Egypt's crops, and on and on. It was a nasty situation, but Pharaoh would not relent.

God will always triumph. But even after all the torture that Pharaoh allowed himself and his people to endure, he still hadn't had enough. Pharaoh said, "I can't compete with God, so I'm going to Plan B. Since I can't challenge God, I'm going to compromise His people." God told Moses to demand that Pharaoh let His people journey into the wilderness to worship Him. Whenever the devil realizes that he can't challenge God, he starts trying to get God's people to settle for less than God intended them to have. Knowing he can't defeat God, the devil starts opening negotiations, trying to get God's people to compromise.

God does not bless us half-heartedly, and the devil knows that. God blesses His people wholistically. God wants to bless the totality of our lives. We sometimes circumvent God's plans for us by settling for less than God has in mind. God wants to give some woman a company of her own, but she doesn't have confidence in herself, so she settles for being a vice president of minority affairs for someone else. That's a compromise. Do not settle for a job with a company if God intends for you to have an entire company of your own. Some people make compromises in their personal lives. Many Christians are living beneath their potential, not taking advantage of the tremendous possibilities God has in store. God wants to give some man a good wife, but he doesn't think he looks good enough or makes enough money, so he settles for a kind of woman other than what he wants. People stay in relationships they never should have been in at all because they don't think they can do any better. They put up with abuse, infidelity, disrespect, or settle for a partner who is only willing to give 10 percent to the relationship instead of 100 percent. There is no reason for God's children to settle for second best. We serve a first-class God who gives first-class blessings. He sent a first-class Savior who died a first-class death on the cross, had

Many Christians are living beneath their potential, not taking advantage of the tremendous possibilities God has in store.

a first-class resurrection, sent a first-class Holy Ghost, and is coming back with a first-class Second Coming.

As a part of his compromise plan, Pharaoh summoned Moses and said, "Go sacrifice to God in the land." But that was not what God demanded. God wanted them out of Egypt. Likewise, God wants each of us to come out of the Egypt that binds us. The devil wanted to convince Moses that the people could stay in Egypt and worship the true God—as a compromise. But God said, "No compromise." Israel could not worship in Egypt because there is no such thing as a part-time slave. They would never be free as long as they remained in Egypt. No one can coexist in Canaan and Egypt. We can't live in Canaan and work in Egypt. We can't live in Egypt and worship in Canaan. That's part-time slavery—not good enough for God's people. God tells us to get out of our Egypt—out of our nicotine, our alcohol, our adultery, our addictions—all the way out.

In Exodus 8:28 Pharaoh said, "I will let you go and offer sacrifices to the Lord your God in the desert, but you must not go very far." That's just a compromise, because God said to get all the way out of Egypt. God wanted His people so far away from Egypt that He put a sea between them so that Pharaoh would no longer trouble them. God wants us far away from our Egypt. He wants to put an ocean between us and the thing that binds us, but some of us will not walk away.

Whatever Egypt is to a person, God says, "Get far away from it." But Egypt keeps saying, "You can go, but just don't go too far." That's when it is time to say, "I'm

No one can coexist in Canaan and Egypt. We can't live in Canaan and work in Egypt. We can't live in Egypt and worship in Canaan.

through with So-and-So." It is also time to take So-and-So's name out of the Rolodex®. Singer R Kelly has a song that says, "When a woman's fed up, ain't nothing you can do about it." When we're really fed up with bad habits and bad influences, we want to be rid of every trace, every evidence, and every temptation associated with our Egypt. The devil doesn't mind us getting away from Egypt for a little while; he just doesn't want us to go too far. When we go too far away from Egypt, that means we've ventured over into the Promised Land—the land of God's blessings. That is how many Christians are when it comes to Jesus. The devil doesn't mind if we go to church, but he doesn't want us to go too far with it. We can come and hear a good sermon, say some amens, and even shout a little, but he wants us to leave church and go right back to Egypt—back to that addiction, back to eating foods that are slowly killing us, back to that sugar daddy or that sweet thang on the side, back to stealing from the company, back to abusing our children.

After we leave church and go back to living in Egypt, Satan is encouraging us, "Be real, Child. You gotta live in the real world. That preacher don't know what he's talking about. You can't pay your bills if you quit seeing that married man." He wants us to think that we cannot give up the lifestyle we live in Egypt. To keep us from becoming too frustrated, he compromises by telling Christians to go on to church and praise the Lord, just as long as we come back to Egypt when it's over. The devil doesn't want us to get too serious about religion. He doesn't want us to get carried away by doing things like serving in the church, coming to Bible study, paying our tithes, and engaging in personal prayer and devotion. When the devil thinks we're going too far, he starts telling us things like, "Man, you don't have to keep going to church all the time. You're taking this thing too far." Or he'll attack us in a different way, "Why are you tithing when you don't even have enough money to pay your own bills? God doesn't expect you to do that. You're taking it too far now."

When the devil starts telling us that we are going too far, we need to tell him, "Well, Jesus went too far for me. He went all the way to Calvary for me when I was a sinner and couldn't help myself." We need to tell Satan, "He went too far for me when He delivered me from my enemies, 'cause He didn't have to do it. He went too far when He delivered me from drug addiction, 'cause He didn't have to do it." When the Lord has delivered us—no compromises, no conditions—we have to take it far!

Moses was unwilling to compromise God's people, and God delivered them from Egypt, although it cost Pharaoh his first-born son. We know that three days after the Israelites left, Pharaoh had a change of heart and went after them to bring them back. When Israel saw the Red Sea in front of them and Pharaoh's mighty army charging behind them, they complained to Moses, "Why did you bring us out here to die?"

Whenever we seem backed into a corner for serving God, we need to remember that the Lord doesn't bring us out of bondage into defeat. The Lord brings us out to show us great and marvelous things. He sometimes puts us in situations where we don't know what to do so that He can show off, flex His muscles. We only discover God's healing power after we get sick. We don't understand God's blessing power until He puts food in an empty refrigerator. He can't put money in our pockets until we're dead broke. Israel would never have known God's power if they hadn't been caught between Pharaoh

Whenever we seem backed into a corner for serving God, we need to remember that the Lord doesn't bring us out of bondage into defeat.

and the Red Sea. Through his walk with the Lord, Moses gained empowerment. Gone was the stumbling, stuttering man who stood at the burning bush. The Moses who emerged out of faithfulness was a man who knew that God would see them through. And through Moses' empowerment, God's people were empowered. As God's people stood by the Red Sea, Moses told them, "Be still, and watch the Lord fight your battle." Sometimes we just have to be still and let the Lord do His work. When the Lord did His work that day at the Red Sea, over 600,000 marched toward freedom on dry land. When Pharaoh's army tried to follow them, the whole host was drowned.

God wants to bless His people. He wants to deliver His people. Satan wants to keep us bound in Egypt. But we have to be willing to stand firm and say, "No compromise. If you take my house, no compromise. If you take my spouse, no compromise. If you take my job, no compromise. Go ahead, devil, and repossess my car. Give me a pink slip on my job. Put my child in jail. No matter what you do, I refuse to compromise. I'm standing on the promises of God, my Savior." Through our refusal to give in to Satan's compromise, we gain empowerment. Each time we say no to Egypt and keep heading toward Canaan, we become stronger in the Lord. Moses came a long way from changing a stick into a serpent to using that same stick to part a great sea.

We serve an uncompromising God, and He wants us to stand firm. That's why the apostle Paul admonishes us in Ephesians 6:11 to "put on the whole armor of God, that you may be able to stand against the wiles of the devil" (NKJV). When we stand in Him, the Lord makes a way.

Each time we say no to Egypt and keep heading toward Canaan, we become stronger in the Lord.

God made a way for Israel through Moses. When Moses walked up to the burning bush, he began a walk of empowerment. He went to the bush fumbling in his speech, not thinking very much of himself, and trying to shy away from doing anything of importance. Plus, he had a murder rap hanging over his head. But he started walking with the Lord. The longer he walked, the stronger he became. The Lord empowered Moses, and through him delivered a nation to freedom.

If we want power from God, we must be willing to keep walking. We probably won't start where we think we should, but Moses didn't either. We can't just look at how Moses ended up; we must look at how he started. We may not be able to see why in the world God would want to use us to do anything significant. Moses couldn't. We may stumble and fumble a few times. Moses did. But we must keep walking. And somehow our faithfulness and obedience become a walk of empowerment. We look back—like Moses' experience—and see how far the Lord has brought us.

When the trumpets sounded, the people shouted, and at the sound of the trumpet, when the people gave a loud shout, the wall collapsed; so every man charged straight in, and they took the city.

VICTORY

Joshua 5:13—6:20

Joshua faced a seemingly impossible task. He was charged to take down the wall of a heavily fortified city. By following the Lord's instruction, Joshua was able to lead God's people to victory. Because he allowed the Lord to guide him instead of trying to make his own way, Joshua experienced victory as he went with the Lord.

Joshua is one of the most intriguing personalities of the Bible, because Joshua and his generation were given the awesome task of moving Israel into Canaan, the Land of Promise, after 40 years of wandering in the wilderness. When we think about Canaan, we use it metaphorically to refer to our eternal home. Heaven is depicted as Canaan in many hymns. Canaan and heaven are synonymous symbolically. But Canaan is not truly heaven, because when Israel moved into Canaan they had problems. In the real heaven, there will be no more problems. Someone called heaven "No More," because there are no more problems, no more headaches, no more suffering or pain there. Battles still had to be fought in Canaan. When we get to heaven, there will be no more battles.

When Joshua took his men over the Jordan River and they set their feet on Canaan, the Land of Promise, the first battle they had to fight was the Battle of Jericho. We are familiar with the Negro Spiritual about Joshua and the Battle of Jericho. Joshua fought the battle of Jericho, and the walls came tumbling down. While we know the song, there are some spiritual principles to be learned about how the walls of Jericho came down. We all have some Jerichos in our lives. We all have some impregnable fortress, something in our way, preventing us from possessing our Promised Land. And so it was with Israel. If they couldn't get past Jericho, they would never be able to possess the land of Canaan.

Jericho was a city of antiquity. Its place was great in antiquity because it is the oldest inhabited city in the world. There is no known city in the world older than Jericho. It is a beautiful, sunny city, a vacation spot. Not only was Jericho a city of great antiquity even in Joshua's day, it also was a city of great iniquity. Sin ran rampant in Jericho. They didn't blush in Jericho. Sin was not done in the back streets; it was paraded down Main Street. They had everything, they had HBO — Hell's Box Office—and it was open day and night.

Jericho also was a fortified city. It was impregnable because thick walls protected the city. Joshua 6:1 says that the gates of Jericho were kept shut and guarded to keep the Israelites out. No one could enter or leave the city. In the Bible, such cities are known as strongholds. Not only do nations have cities that are strongholds, like Jericho, but there are strongholds in our lives also. We are walking Jerichos because we have strongholds. A stronghold is something that a person can't get out of or into: nothing in, nothing out; nothing out, nothing in.

There are some situations that we get into and can't get out of—problems, bad habits, bad relationships, and bad feelings. There are some habits that we don't want and don't even like, but we're in it—it's a stronghold. Some people have been trying to break free from their stronghold for years. Some people are trying to get love in their

A stronghold is something that a person can't get out of or into: nothing in, nothing out; nothing out, nothing in.

lives but it won't come in. Some people are bent on self-destruction because of a stronghold that won't let the truth in. Still, some people won't even let the Gospel in because the devil has put up a stronghold in their lives. For example, our nation and communities have been dealing with cocaine and crack as a medical problem, and it is. But it goes much deeper. The problem is a spiritual, demonic stronghold that the devil does not want addicts to get out of. Some addicts have been going to the clinic when they really need to come to church. Victory over our strongholds, our personal Jerichos, is brought down only through faith.

How did Jericho come down? The walls came down through faith. When the New Testament writers looked back at how the walls came down, Hebrews 11:30 says that faith toppled them. It is faith that makes the walls of addiction fall down. Faith can make the walls of personal problems fall down. Faith can make the walls of poverty fall down. Faith can make the walls of isolation, failure, and hopelessness fall down. The only way that we can experience victory and cause some walls to fall down in our lives is by exercising faith. Walls come down through faith— not with money, not by taking advice from friends, and not through calling Mama or Daddy. When we grow up we begin to understand that Mama and Daddy have strongholds in their own lives. The only way to gain victory over our strongholds is through the personal exercise of faith; but not just any kind of faith. Believers must have the right kind of faith if we want walls to come tumbling down in our lives.

The only way that we can experience victory and cause some walls to fall down in our lives is by exercising faith.

Joshua 5:13 says, "While Joshua was in Jericho he suddenly saw a man in front of him holding a sword. Joshua went to him and asked him 'Are you one of our soldiers or are you an enemy?'" In other words, Joshua was asking, "Are you with Israel, or are you with Jericho?"

"'Neither,' the man answered. "I am here as the commander of the Lord's army."

When we think about our problems constantly, the devil just adds more fuel to them so they get bigger and bigger until they become over-whelming.

Joshua threw himself on the ground and worshiped saying, "I am your servant, Sir. What do you want me to do?" Joshua was outside looking at Jericho because Jericho was in his way. Jericho was his obstacle, so he was looking at the city, sizing it up. He must have been thinking, "How am I possibly going to get around this? How is this going to be moved out of our way?" He just kept looking at it.

All of us probably have felt that way at some point in our lives. When we are facing an obstacle, we spend nights, days, and weeks just thinking about our Jericho. It occupies and dominates the mind. Naturally, any problem a person thinks about all the time is bound to get bigger. When we think about our problems constantly, the devil just adds more fuel to them so they get bigger and bigger until they become overwhelming. Then the problem seems impossible to solve—even for God.

The more Joshua looked at Jericho, the bigger the walls got. And the bigger they got, the more impenetrable they got. He couldn't go through them and he couldn't get around them. The walls didn't move; they just loomed larger. As he stood and stared at the fortress, Joshua suddenly realized that he was not alone. Someone was standing near him. Most people have had a sneaking suspicion that somebody was with them, even when no one else was standing near. Joshua looked up and saw a soldier standing with his sword drawn and up in the air. Seeing the soldier postured for battle, Joshua inquired about the man's loyalty. The man must have looked like a skilled warrior, a powerful foe for anyone who came up against him. Who was this holding the sword? This man was Jesus in His pre-incarnate state. The Son of God would pop up periodically in the Old Testament before He was born in Bethlehem. Another instance is when He delivered Shadrach, Meshach, and Abednego from the fiery furnace.

There He was with Joshua while the troubled leader examined his problem. Joshua was looking at his problem, but the minute he bowed down to Jesus, Jericho was no longer Joshua's problem, it was the Lord's problem. When God's children bow down in prayer and praise, their problem then becomes His problem. We have to tell the God of our salvation, "I'm going to worship You and depend on You to move my Jericho out of the way!"

But there will be some Jerichos that we are not smart enough to move. There will be other Jerichos that we do not have enough money to move. In fact, God lets Jerichos come into our lives sometimes so that we will quit tripping off our egos and start realizing that we do not have the power to battle Jericho alone. With Jesus as Captain, we've already got the victory. Before we even know it, those walls are coming down. We live in time, but God lives in eternity. We live today, but we don't know what's going to happen tomorrow. In God, yesterday, today, and tomorrow are all taking place at the same time. Whatever is happening tomorrow is happening today in the mind of God.

God told Joshua, "I'm the Captain and here's the battle strategy. I want you to get the troops and the people and march around Jericho one time for six straight days. I don't want you to say anything, just march once daily. On the seventh day, I want you to march around seven times. And after you march around the seventh time, I want you to shout and start praising Me and see what happens to the walls."

Well, those are some strange orders. It is not humanly possible to march down walls that are large enough to fortify a city. To bring down walls we think we need battering rams and some kind of scaffolding. We think we need arrows shooting through the air and ladders scaling up the walls. But God told Joshua, "No, I don't want you to do that. I just want you to walk around the problem, once daily for six days. And I don't want you to say anything."

The people in Jericho must have been looking at the Israelites, laughing at them, saying, "You are fools to try and obey this kind of crazy strategy." While the people of Jericho were taunting them, they were forbidden to speak a word. People make fun of us today and call us crazy because we follow the Lord, but we can't worry about that. Instead of worrying about that and getting sidetracked, all we have to do is just keep on marching. Too often, we want God to make sense. But God doesn't have to make sense. In spiritual matters, we're dumb. We don't know right from wrong, up from down, sanity from insanity. We don't know the right way to go. God's ways are not our ways.

I know that I don't understand the ways of God, but I don't understand a whole lot of things. I don't understand how a brown cow can eat green grass and produce

People make fun of us today and call us crazy because we follow the Lord, but we can't worry about that.

white milk that turns into yellow butter. I don't understand why God wants me to walk around my Jericho without uttering a sound. In fact, I don't understand why God wants me to do many of the things that He wants me to do. But it doesn't have to make sense. I've decided that I'm just going to comply with what the Lord says do. I'm going to keep on marching. It's important to keep on marching, even when nothing happens. Nothing happened the first day that Israel marched around the walls of Jericho. Nothing happened on the second day, or the third day, or the fourth day, or the fifth day, or the sixth day. That's important because a whole lot of people would have given up by the sixth day—just when God was about to break through.

That's why we have to wait on Him. We have to keep on marching. And that's all Israel did. Folks were laughing at them, but they kept marching. People laugh at Christians for coming to church, Bible in hand, no money, and no mate. Let them laugh. We have to keep on marching. We have to keep on marching around the problem and doing what the Lord said do.

Israel kept marching until the seventh day. On the seventh day, they marched one time, a second time, and on and on until the sixth time. When they marched around the seventh time, Joshua said, "Blow the trumpet and everybody shout!" When they began to shout, no walls had come down yet. The battle had not yet been won, but they shouted anyway. We don't have to wait until the walls come down before we shout. We need to shout in anticipation of what we know the Lord is getting ready to do.

We don't have to wait until the walls come down before we shout. We need to shout in anticipation of what we know the Lord is getting ready to do.

– 55 –

People don't understand God's scope. Whether we are broke, in trouble, sick, heartbroken, or bearing heavy burdens, we can still shout. We don't have to wait until we see our blessing to shout, because we know that if the Lord said it's going to happen, it's going to happen. Some of us wait until we get in church to shout. But sometimes when we're on the job, or at home, or in the car, we've got to shout because we know the walls are getting ready to come down. While we're shouting some unbelievers may look at us and ask, "Why don't you shut up?" But we can't worry about that. We have to shout and praise God from the heart as we watch the Captain of our army at work.

We just have to trust God to bring down the walls that block us from moving forward.

At the seventh revolution the people shouted. At their shout there came a shaking in Jericho. The walls started coming down, brick by brick. When we see bricks come down, we need to shout. We don't have to wait until the wall comes down completely. When we see the first brick tumble we need to shout, "Thank You!" When the whole wall comes down, we need to stand on top of it and shout, "Thank You! Thank You! You brought down my wall!" When we allow God to be the Captain, we don't have the problem any more. It then belongs to God. We just have to trust God to bring down the walls that block us from moving forward.

After Israel won that battle, they faced another one. They won the next battle too, because they allowed God to lead them. In battle after battle they allowed God to lead them so they had victory after victory.

The Christian life is like that, too—one battle after another. There's no such thing as a battle-free Christian. The devil is going to make sure of that. Satan is always going to find some way to pull us into spiritual battle. Once we get the kids straight, then our spouse starts acting crazy. And when we get our personal life straight, it gets crazy at the job. Once we get the job straight, some unexpected bill pops up. Once we get the bill paid, here comes something else. If it ain't one thing, it's another. We just need to let God come on in.

When we are faced with a Jericho, we are faced with three choices:

1. We can stand gaping at the thick, high, seemingly impenetrable walls and declare, "Oh, I can't take it!"

2. We can run back into the wilderness. Fear and faithlessness have driven many a frustrated Christian back to the wilderness. If Canaan symbolizes victory, and Egypt means slavery, the wilderness represents the land of Christian frustration.

3. We can stand in faith and let God lead. When we allow Him to guide us, the Lord will give us victory.

But those who hope in the LORD will renew their strength. They will soar on wings like eagles; they will run and not grow weary, They will walk and not be faint.

Isaiah 40:31, NIV

Renewal

Isaiah 40:21-31

God's people were weary and worn, and so was His prophet. Through his reliance on the promise and power of the living God, Isaiah experienced divine renewal and encouraged God's people to know that the Lord would renew their strength.

A young seminary-trained pastor was assuming his first pastoral charge in a community that was filled with problems. It was an urban neighborhood that was experiencing many of the social pathologies that we have come to associate with high-crime areas. It was a neighborhood filled with drugs, prostitution, illiteracy, and the accompanying moods of hopelessness and despair. This young, idealistic seminary graduate toured the neighborhood and saw firsthand the drugs dealers and the women whose self-esteem was so low that they were selling their bodies on the street. This young man of God was heartbroken by what he witnessed. As tears began to run down his cheeks one of the deacons who had been in the church for many years looked to the young pastor and said, "Reverend, I know it's a bad community. But cheer up, Pastor, you will get used to it."

There are certain realities in life. Jesus told His disciples that the poor will always be among us (Matthew 26:11). And in 2,000 years His words have not been proven wrong. Despite these realities, there are some things in life that we should never get used to. We should never get used to ignorance. We should never get used to abject poverty, prostitution, drugs, and hopelessness. We should never accommodate and acclimate ourselves to evil, whether systemic or personal.

But in order to get through life, all of us manage to get used to something. Some if not all of us have accommodated ourselves to something that is less than desirable. For some, it is a dead-end job. Others accommodate the unloving attitude of a spouse or family member because it seems easier than confronting the situation. Ask yourself: To what circumstances in my life and in the lives of my children have I said, "Well, I'll just get used to it"?

God does not want us to adjust to everything that comes our way. There are some times when we can't do any better than our present circumstances. During the times when we can't do any better, we need the spirit of contentment. Paul was in jail and couldn't get out, so he wrote to the church at Philippi and said, "I have learned to be content whatever the circumstances (Philippians 4:11). Paul contented himself with being in jail because at that moment he couldn't do any better.

We should never be content when we can do better. Every morning we get up and look in the mirror. What do we see? We see something tore up, right? If we smile there are little particles between our teeth, that is, if we've still got teeth. And as we keep looking we notice particles of dried mucus formed in the crevices of our eyes. And sometimes there are runs on the side of the mouth after a night of "slobbering" in our sleep. Our hair is disheveled. That's what we see in the morning—all of us.

None of us wakes up and goes to the mirror with it all together. It takes some doing before we are presentable and can leave the house. Never do we look in the mirror and say, "That's okay. I'll be content with my messed-up hair and crust in my eyes. I'll just be content with bad breath." We are not content with our appearance as soon as we get out of bed. We do not adjust ourselves to what we see in the mirror first thing in the morning because we know that we can improve on it. And so we grab our toothbrush, turn on the shower, and comb our hair. We take action because we do not like what the mirror shows. We look in the mirror and say, "I gotta make some improvements."

God never wants us to adjust to anything that diminishes us and that is beneath us. He does not want us to adjust to abuse. He does not want us to adjust to ignorance and poverty. We cannot simply adjust to some of the habits of some of our young African Americans by saying, "Well, that's just the way they are." Rather, we must insist that they make some adjustments like: "Pull your pants up and make some adjustments, son. Clean up your language, make some adjustments. It's time to improve your grades. Make some adjustments!"

In Isaiah 40, the prophet is angry because the people of God had accommodated themselves to the idea of and contented themselves with the reality of being a captive people. They were living beneath their privilege and possibilities. Isaiah wrote to them saying, "What's wrong with you? Why are you living as captives in Babylon?" They were living as captives because they underestimated the power of God. They did not live as though they knew the God of power. Because God has power, His children do not have to adjust to anything. Because God has power, His people don't have to simply accept anything. If we believe that we serve a God of power, sometimes we ought to be cocky, bold, and confronting. If, as God's people, we are abused on the job, we can simply say, "Well I don't have to take this. God's got other plans for me." If a child of God is just being strung along year after

If we believe that we serve a God of power, sometimes we ought to be cocky, bold, and confronting.

year in a relationship that has no future, that child can say, "I don't have to take this. My God has power!"

But the people were behaving as though they did not know God has power, so Isaiah had to remind them about His power. They needed to be reminded and renewed in their relationship with God. Repeatedly in Isaiah 40 he asks them, "Have you not heard? Have you not known? Have you not understood about the power of God?" It is important to remember that Isaiah's questions are filled with sarcasm. To ask these Jews, "Have you not heard about God?" is really an indictment, because it is through the Jews that we have come to know the true and living God. It is through the Jewish faith that we have come to grasp monotheism. It is through the Jews that we have come to know what is called the Shema: "Hear O Israel: the Lord thy God is one God" (Deuteronomy 6:4). It is through the Jews that a man named Moses imparted to us the Decalogue. It is through the Jews that we have the prophets, both major and minor. Yet, having passed down all of this knowledge and wisdom, Isaiah had to ask these descendants of Israel, who for generations had known of Jehovah-Jireh, Jehovah-Nissi, Jehovah-Rapha, and Jehovah-Tsidkenu, "Have you heard? Have you not known?"

Isaiah's question to the Jews is akin to someone asking Bill Gates, "Have you not heard about computers?" It would be like asking Michael Jordan, "Have you not heard about basketball?" Asking Tiger Woods, "Do you not know? Have you not heard about golf?" would be no less sarcastic. Golf is synonymous with Tiger Woods, as basketball is synonymous with Michael Jordan and com-

But the people were behaving as though they did not know God has power, so Isaiah had to remind them about His power.

puters with Bill Gates. In a like manner, belief in Yahweh was associated with the Jews, His chosen people. Yet they were acting like there is no God. So Isaiah had to ask them if they had ever heard about God and His power.

And the same question is relevant for Christians today who feel defeated by life's challenges. I have to ask them, "Have you not heard about God?" Anyone who thinks that there is no future needs to be asked, "Have you not heard? Have you not understood about God?" For the Christian community the question could be expanded to, "Did you not know that the same God who raised Jesus Christ from the dead has power to help you in your life?" For anybody who thinks that he or she cannot overcome a mountain in his or her way needs to answer the question: "Have you not heard? Have you not understood?" It is amazing that Christians come to church week after week, listen to the singing Sunday after Sunday, and hear the preached Word, but go out after the benediction like they have not experienced the power of God. We need to live daily in the knowledge that there is a God who sits high and has all power. This everlasting God majors in helping those who are weak. He's great. He's awesome. There are no words to describe the greatness of the God we serve.

When manufacturers want to get their products on the market they get the Madison Avenue giants to create a slogan for a particular product that highlights its merits. Tide™, the advertisers said, gets the dirt out. Well, God gets the dirt out of souls that are unclean. They told us Coke™ is the real thing. But God is the Real Thing. Clairol® says that VO5™ hairspray holds in all kinds of weather. God holds His children together in all kinds of weather. Scotch™ tape seems invisible when it really is there. The God we serve is there even though we can't see Him. Our God possesses power and, moreover, He provides what He possesses. He wants to give us some power. Acts 1:8 says, "But you will receive power when the Holy Spirit comes on you; and you will be my witnesses in Jerusalem, and in all Judea and Samaria, and to the ends of the earth."

We will never have so much money that we won't need God's power. We'll never be so enlightened, so cultured that we won't need God's power. Because we get weak in body and in mind, we need to be renewed by God's power. We get sick and tired and we need God's power to give us the strength to keep going. Sometimes the tiredness is not physical; sometimes it is emotional, mental, or even spiritual. Sometimes we get tired of having to go through the same things over and over again, things we thought we had resolved five years ago, but that same old problem just won't seem to go away. Sometimes we get so tired that we feel like we have nothing else to give. We've given all that we have and we ask ourselves, "What more do my children want me to do?" "What more does my spouse want from me?" "What more does my employer expect of me?" Meanwhile, the bills pile up, leaving us feeling overwhelmed. That's when we have to recognize that God gives power to the weak. He will share His power with His people. That is why Paul said, "I can do all things through Christ who strengthens me" (Philippians 4:13). He says that if we wait on the Lord, the one who possesses power will produce power.

When Isaiah says "wait on the Lord," he doesn't mean idleness or inactivity. Waiting on the Lord doesn't mean we just twiddle our thumbs. The prophet doesn't want us to passively and nonchalantly wait for something to happen. The word wait in Hebrew is the same word that we use in English for what takes place when we go to a restaurant. We go out to eat and there's somebody called a waiter who will give us a menu. The waiter comes to the table where we are seated and serves us from the beginning of the meal until the end. Waiters will bring water then take the food order. They take the order to the kitchen and submit it. Then they serve the food, and keep coming back to the table periodically just to make sure everything is okay.

Waiters worth their tips do not just sit back and do nothing when a diner takes a seat. There is plenty of work for the waiter to do.

Isaiah says if we want to be renewed by God's power, we need to be waiters. Those who wait are those who serve the Lord. That is why Solomon says to come before His presence with singing and before in His courts with praise (Psalm 100). If we want renewed strength, we must serve Him with gladness. And if we serve Him, He has made a promise that He will renew our strength. It is a difficult concept for the human brain to comprehend. It's a human mystery that the more we serve the Lord the stronger we become. The more we praise Him, the more we are renewed.

Our enslaved forebears knew the importance of praising God and serving Him in spite of the inhumane conditions they endured. Many more of us would have been in mental institutions had it not been for the Lord on our side. With today's many and varied pressures—bills, kids, work demands, and other problems—yesterday, today, and tomorrow—many of us shouldn't have the energy to get out of bed. Yet for reasons unknown to the world, we go back out there when Monday morning comes and the alarm clock goes off, and we know we have to deal with some ditch diggers who mean us no good. For some reason that escapes the world, we have the energy and strength to prevail. It didn't come from going to a spa. It didn't come at the hands of a masseuse. It can't be bought at the mall. It can't be earned through a degree from Oxford. Yet, this mysterious Source imparts energy for us to go back out with our strength renewed.

It's a human mystery that the more we serve the Lord the stronger we become. The more we praise Him, the more we are renewed.

The Lord will renew our faith and our strength, and He has promised to constantly resupply our strength in three ways. But first, He makes a condition; He said, "If you wait on Me...." God said, "I will give you strength so that you can mount up on the wings of an eagle." That's our first supply—ecstasy. When we wait on the Lord, sometimes things will go so well, and we are so blessed that things will just overwhelm us. Blessings come, doors swing open; that's ecstasy. We mount up on wings like eagles and soar. We experience blessed bliss.

Sometimes we're not flying, but we're still doing pretty well. God said that sometimes our strength might be renewed so that we can "run and not be weary." We are running smoothly and effortlessly, so we experience our second supply—excitement. Sometimes we are flying; that's ecstasy. Sometimes we are running; that's excitement. But there is a third level. Sometimes we will "walk and not faint," and that's our third supply—endurance. Sometimes God gives us ecstasy. Sometimes He gives us excitement. Sometimes He gives us endurance for the journey.

I do not understand Isaiah. The order of God's renewal seems reversed. It seems as though we are having declining strength instead of ascending strength. Isaiah has us start by mounting up like an eagle. Then he has us to slow down so we can run and not get weary. Finally, Isaiah says that we will walk and not faint. That is a descending progression. It seems that Isaiah should have started us off with a walk, and if we stick with the Lord, we will begin to run. Then, if we keep on walking in obedience to the Lord, we'll fly. But Isaiah didn't say that. He says we will fly, then run, and at last, we will walk.

Why does Isaiah end with walking? Why didn't he get us excited by ending with ecstasy? Because 99 percent of our lives will not be spent in ecstasy. Ninety-nine percent of our lives is not going to be exciting. Most of life is going to be dealing with problems and troubles, not ecstasy. There is no ecstasy in trouble, and there is no excitement about dealing with mundane problems. Most of our life is spent dealing with issues. Do married people thank God for those moments of ecstasy? Not even the best marriage is continuous, uninterrupted ecstasy. Many people don't stay married because they have this fantasy that every day is supposed to be spent caught up in rapture with their spouse. Sometimes marriage is boring. Sometimes marriage is uninspiring.

Then there's the job. Every day on the job is not ecstasy. It certainly isn't exciting all of the time. Some days it's routine, mundane, and we want to be any place but there. Some of us go to these popular Christian conferences and get jacked up. We leave there thinking that we are always supposed to be jacked up and that every moment of every day is supposed to be spent flying like an eagle. Life is not like that. Sometimes life gets rough and messy. But God has promised that even on those bad days when we have neither ecstasy money, nor an ecstasy spouse, nor an ecstasy job, He will renew us by giving us the power to keep on walking. He will give us the power to walk and not faint. He will give us the power to not give up, because contrary to what some Christian teachers espouse, every day is not supposed to be spent in the clouds.

That kind of teaching is not the Judeo-Christian faith. That's new age religion. Everything that the televangelists are preaching on television is not authentic. Some of it is counterfeit Gospel. Some of my brothers and sisters in ministry want people to think faith means that nobody is supposed to get sick, and everybody is supposed to be a

He will give us the power to not give up, because contrary to what some Christian teachers espouse, every day is not supposed to be spent in the clouds.

millionaire. As wonderful as that may seem, it is not true—and it is certainly not real life. Moses experienced ecstasy at the Red Sea, but it wasn't like that every day. He was in the heat of the wilderness for 40 years, sometimes with nothing to eat. Sometimes there was nothing to drink. Sometimes there were people complaining no matter how hard he tried. But because God was with Moses, God gave him the power to keep on going, even in the midst of the desert. If we wait on the Lord, He may not snatch us out of the desert, but He'll give us the power to keep on walking in the midst of the desert.

There are a whole lot of Christians playing church. They are playing because things are not all that great. Things are not going that well. Some of us have got heartache and heartbreak. Others of us are sick or in trouble. Some people have a marriage that's falling apart or kids who won't listen. What are we to do? Some Christians still go to a bottle to get relief. Some believers still think they have to smoke something or snort something, trying to get rid of the pain. Others indulge in self-pity and lie in bed and cry. But that is not the way God will see us through. Even though God is with us, He may not move all of our problems away. We have to live like the song says: "Lord, don't move my mountain, but give me the strength to climb." And if He gives us the strength to take one more step, then we ought to say, "Thank You," because we are blessed.

This Scripture has awakened me at night and I pray, "Lord please let me feel Your Spirit. You get the glory, but please, Lord, let me be effective in communicating it to Your people. Let me effectively open the hearts and minds of Your people so that they will know that God's presence is manifested in three ways."

Ecstasy is not to be discounted. It is to be welcomed and expected, but not all the time because that's not what life is like. God can and will make things exciting at times, and we should look forward to and cherish those instances. But it is important that we are geared up for the walk of endurance, knowing that our God will supply us with constant renewal. If we don't have power to deal with problems on routine days on a routine basis, we are not going to make it. But if we wait on the Lord, God will give us the power to make it.

There was a man who sold vacuum cleaners. He went to a rural community and knocked on the door of a woman and said, "I got a vacuum cleaner that will pick up anything in your house." She tried to stop him, but he was an aggressive salesman. He said, "Wait, honey, let me demonstrate. Don't say anything. Let me show you what I mean."

He went over to the fireplace, scooped up some ashes and started dumping them onto the floor. The woman asked, "What are you doing?" He said, "Don't worry, this vacuum cleaner will pick up anything, anything." He finished strewing the ashes on the floor and said, "I tell you what, this vacuum cleaner here will pick up these ashes. If it won't, I will personally eat those ashes." She looked at him and said, "Mister, you'd better get a fork and a spoon and start eating, because we don't have any electricity way out here." It doesn't make any difference how powerful the vacuum cleaner is if there is no power to run it!

We need that power, and God has promised to give it to those who wait on Him. He is the solid foundation that will keep and sustain us, renewing us constantly. Money will fail you and people will too. Only if we build our lives on the eternal Rock of our salvation may we be secure. God will not fail.

"If we are thrown into the blazing furnace, the God we serve is able to save us from it, and he will rescue us from your hand, O king. But even if he does not, we want you to know, O king, that we will not serve your gods or worship the image of gold you have set up."

Daniel 3:18, NIV

DELIVERANCE

Daniel 3

Shadrach, Meshach, and Abednego were faithful Jews, and were unwilling to be compromised regarding their loyalty to God. Because they were steadfast and faithful in their stand as children of God, they experienced God's deliverance as they went.

In churches throughout the land we sing "It Pays to Serve Jesus." And indeed, it does pay to serve Jesus every day, with every fiber of our being. Jesus said that anyone who leaves mother, father, brothers, and sisters for the sake of the Kingdom shall receive in this life and in the world to come. But while it pays definite dividends to serve Jesus, it also costs to serve Him. Salvation is free, but discipleship is costly. It costs every day. At every step along our Christian journey we pay. Part of the cost of serving Jesus is the heat that we experience—the heat of opposition that we encounter because we choose to serve Him. The word for that heat is persecution. A good working definition of persecution is "suffering that is inflicted on individuals or groups because of their fidelity to God, usually with the objective of inducing apostasy or destroying the faith and intimidating the prospective converts."

So, whether we feel the heat singularly or as part of a group, all Christians will experience persecution. We experience suffering because we are loyal to Christ. When we follow Christ, we experience suffering because of our fidelity to God. Our definition has established that persecution has an objective, which is apostasy. Therefore, if we lose something because of Christ, if doors are shut because of our fidelity to Christ, then the goal is to get us to abandon Christ and fall in line with the world. Society demands conformity because no one is supposed to be different. There is an eleventh commandment that says, "Thou shalt not be different." Yet, to be a Christian means that we are different, having been separated from the world. We cannot make a difference for Christ if we are not somehow different.

God's people are "peculiar" (Deuteronomy 14:2), and so we experience persecution because we are peculiarly aligned with the Lord and not with the world. No one experiences this more intensely than a new Christian. Generally, new Christians experience a great deal of joy, but they also experience persecution. The devil is really out to get them before they become too deeply rooted in the Word. That is why the church must always put its arms around new Christians with new member training classes. The church must not forget that when the Lord gave us the Great Commission, He told us to make disciples. That means we cannot simply bring converts into the church and leave them to their own—and Satan's—devices. Newness in Christianity is similar to a person first going to bed. If he lies on the edge of the bed and doesn't roll over to the center, it is easy for him to fall off the bed. If a new Christian stays where he or she first began and moves no closer, and does not grow in the faith, then that believer is more likely to fall away. If we fail to prepare new converts, we neutralize their faith so that they practice nominal Christianity, being Christians in name only. Magnavox® used to have a slogan that said, "The quality goes in before the name goes on." But many times Christians merely get the name on without the quality inside. A nominal Christian's faith is easily intimidated or destroyed.

A look at Hebrews 10:32-33 will illustrate this point more clearly: "Remember those earlier days after you had received the light, when you stood your ground in a great contest in the face of suffering. Sometimes you were publicly exposed to insult and persecution; at other times you stood side by side with those who were so treated." The key word in this passage is publicly. Persecution is most effective when done publicly, to serve as a deterrent for any would-be prospects or converts. Many Christians have felt the heat of persecution because they chose to align themselves with Christ—and not just the martyrs like Joan of Arc. Everyday, ordinary believers experience the heat of persecution on the job, within the family, among friends, and sometimes at the church. Some are persecuted because they go to church on Wednesday night. Others may observe this behavior and say, "You're always up in church." Some believers are persecuted because they believe in tithing, or praying, or because they don't do some of the things they used to do. All a Christian has to do, whether new or mature in the faith, to experience the heat of persecution is to move from the ungodly to the godly.

Living in the B.C. (Before Christ) era of our lives is different from living in the fullness of the Lord. Some are experiencing the heat of persecution because they don't go along to get along anymore. Anyone who moves from being a doormat or a yes person to being a person of strength and maturity through Christ will feel persecution. One would think that others would be happy when we are delivered from low self-esteem, worthlessness, and spiritual poverty. On the contrary, people get angry when they can't walk all over a reformed doormat. They want that old, controllable person back. They punish the converted being for the transformation. They withhold their approval in an attempt to resurrect old insecurities and feelings of inferiority. That is the heat of persecution.

All a Christian has to do, whether new or mature in the faith, to experience the heat of persecution is to move from the ungodly to the godly.

Some people come to church on a bogus promise, believing that by coming to church and praying to God, they won't have to face the heat.

Anyone who has not experienced persecution should engage in some serious self-examination, because it is difficult, if not impossible, for a twice-born person to peacefully coexist with once-born people. The twice born tend not to fit in the culture of once-born people. Therefore, a lack of persecution may indicate a lack of authenticity in one's faith. Contrary to what we feel, persecution may serve as a directional sign that you are on the right road. That is why Jesus tells believers to, "rejoice, and be exceedingly glad" when we face persecutions (Matthew 5:12). Persecution is a sign of authentic Christian faith, because if they did it to Jesus, they'll do it to His believers. The servant is not above the master. In Matthew 10:24-25 Jesus said, "If they did it to me, they'll do it to you, too."

So what does a Christian do when the heat of persecution is on? The third chapter of Daniel suggests that when we are experiencing persecution, we should simply enjoy the heat. In other words, we can't expect God to get us out of the fire every time. Some people come to church on a bogus promise, believing that by coming to church and praying to God, they won't have to face the heat. Those who believe that way will be sorely disappointed. In fact, it may even get worse! There are people who came to church because they were already feeling the heat. Instead of cooling down, however, things got even hotter. The heat may continue for several years. But in the midst of the heat we must remember that God's hand is on the thermostat. God controls the thermostat and regulates the temperature in the furnace. Therefore, if

God doesn't stop the heat, God wants you to find a way to enjoy the heat until deliverance comes.

Is it possible to enjoy the fire when the heat is on? Even Christians may wonder if it is possible to have a "fireproof" faith that does not burn up and fly away as ashes when the heat is turned up high.

The story of Shadrach, Meshach, and Abednego reveals how believers can enjoy the fire when the heat is really on. For the sake of the story, let us consider Shadrach, Meshach, and Abednego as foreign exchange students. As students from Israel, they were brought from Judah to Babylon to serve in King Nebuchadnezzar's court. This Babylonian monarch held one of the greatest empires in human history. But the problem with the Babylonian Empire is similar to that of Canada. A diverse nation, Canada has French-speaking, English-speaking, Spanish-speaking citizens, and more. There is a great deal of cultural diversity there. Like Canada, Babylon was a patchwork quilt culturally, an amalgam of different ethnicities, cultures, and nationalities. Therefore, many inhabitants of Babylon, like Shadrach, Meshach, and Abednego, were not natives.

Diversity is beautiful, but it also creates its own challenges and problems. A diverse population is not easily unified. For example, for most of recent history, large regions of the United States have been comprised of African Americans and European Americans. Over the years our cultures have fused to an extent, despite our differences. But things are changing. For example, in places like Miami, New York, and Los Angeles, there is a great deal of diversity—various West Indian, Latino, and Asian cultures. They speak different languages and have different cultural values, different foods, different interests, and different dialects.

How do leaders unify such diversity? This was the problem confronting the Babylonian Empire. King Nebuchadnezzar decided to unify the nation through religion. Daniel 3:1 opens by explaining that Nebuchadnezzar had a gold statue made that was ninety feet high and nearly nine feet wide and had it set up on the plain of Dura. This golden statue was designed to unify religion. The massive size of the statue reveals something about its purpose. This tall, narrow object of worship was out of balance. What we worship can get us out of balance—emotionally, psychologically, financially, spiritually, or relationally. Our lives are a reflection of what we worship, and if human beings worship the wrong thing or the wrong person, our worship, and therefore our lives, are out of balance. If one imperfect being worships another imperfect being, the worshiper's life is out of balance. The reason a drug addict's life is out of balance is because the drug is the addict's object of worship. We become like what we worship.

If one imperfect being worships another imperfect being, the worshiper's life is out of balance.

Nebuchadnezzar's statue was out of balance because the king himself was out of balance. Everybody who worshiped this statue would be out of balance. What Nebuchadnezzar wanted is called eclecticism—he wanted to merge religions. He wanted to mix everything and bring everybody's religion into the picture. Today, the movement that attempts to fuse all religious tenets is called New Age religion. The New Age religion is an attempt to take some Islam, some Christianity, some Hinduism, some Buddhism, and some ancient religions and stir it all together to create one eclectic religion. But a Christian can't be eclectic; however, we can be ecumenical. There's a difference.

Being ecumenical means having a cooperative relationship with other religions or religious denominations. That means a Christian can co-exist with the brothers in the Nation of Islam. When I see the brothers of the Nation on the street, I am polite. I speak and, periodically, I even buy a newspaper from them. I have friends who are members of the Nation of Islam. Brothers of the Nation of Islam used to come to St. Stephen Baptist Church and listen to me preach. But that is where the blending ended, because I can't blend the crescent with the cross. I can't blend the Koran with the Holy Bible. I can't blend Mohammed with Jesus. They believe that Mohammad is superior to Jesus. For them, Mohammad is the chief prophet. But I believe that there is only one way and that's Jesus Christ—the Way, the Truth, and the Life.

There is a movement among certain theological liberals that is trying to prevent Christians from witnessing to people of other faiths. That movement says, "Don't be a religion imperialist and impose your faith on other folks." But in Matthew 28:19-20 Jesus commands us to share our faith with others.

Another reason that Nebuchadnezzar's statue was out of balance is because this 9-foot by 90-foot icon was set up in Dura, where the Jewish peasants lived. Of course, the Jews were forbidden by their laws to bow down to anything other than God. They were not supposed to worship a graven image like the one the king had set up in Dura. That was the equivalent of erecting a statue of Bull Conner or George Wallace in Harlem.

To ensure that they worshiped the statue, Nebuchadnezzar's herald proclaimed that at the sound of the horn, flute, zither, lyre, harp, pipes and all kinds of music, every person of every nationality and religion was to bow to the golden statue. Anyone who failed to comply with the law would be thrown into a blazing furnace. The word herald may be interpreted "preacher," so Nebuchadnezzar had a preacher on the payroll who went around announcing what they must do. This passage also demonstrates that preachers have to be careful not to become puppets or prophets for the government. The king also used music to get the people excited about their worship. Nebuchadnezzar hired a preacher and the Babylonian philharmonic to manipulate the people. Nebuchadnezzar got the best musicians to lull the people into doing what God had forbidden. Obviously, the king knew what he was doing. As soon as the music started, the people knew that all they had to do was bow down and worship. The music was so alluring that they forgot they were bowing down to a false, unbalanced god.

Music can be used as a tool to lift believers to God, or it can be used as a tool to take them down to hell. It has been said that you can always tell what a people are thinking socially by what they are singing musically. That is a powerful statement. People are influenced by music. That's why there is always music playing in stores; music puts people in a spending mood. One day I went over to my neighbor's house and he had one of my favorite songs playing, "Five, ten, fifteen, twenty, twenty-five, thirty years of love. Are you happy? Ooh, Ooooh." Immediately, I was right back in the 70s, with my bell bottom pants and all of that stuff! Whoever writes the music of the nation determines the morals of the nation. Our African American leaders have advocated watching various industries that have had an adverse effect on our people. But little has been said about the music that is coming out of our Babylon and influencing our kids. So, when people want to know why black people don't have respect for each other, it is because we sing about disrespect. It is the same reason we don't respect our women. Our music has contributed to this tendency among young blacks to want to be thugs and "gangstas;" their music glorifies thug boys and gangsta life.

With all that the king did to fortify his efforts to bring about religious unity, Nebuchadnezzar's command was impossible to obey, because authentic worship cannot be mandated. If worship is authentic, it is not the result of coercion or force. Worship is internal. You don't have to command people to worship. Nevertheless, the king put things in motion, blindly believing that he had legislated unified worship in the land.

After the king's decree, some Babylonian astrologers seized the opportunity to denounce the Jews, three in particular. They said, "O Nebuchadnezzar, may your majesty live forever. Your majesty has issued an order that as soon as Snoop Dogg gets ready, everyone is to bow down and worship the unbalanced idol. And that anyone who does not bow down and worship is to be thrown into a blazing furnace. But there are some Jews that you put in charge of the province of Babylon who are ignoring your decree."

The reason they were telling on Shadrach, Meshach, and Abednego was because they were in charge. Had Shadrach, Meshach, and Abednego been the kind of brothers who did nothing more than hang out on the street corner, we never would have heard about them. But the Lord had blessed them to be in charge. The Lord had elevated them, and anytime the Lord elevates His people, there will always be "playa haters" and "crazy makers" who are willing to do anything and everything to try to bring them down. "The higher the level, the greater the devil."

...anytime the Lord elevates His people, there will always be "playa haters" and "crazy makers" who are willing to do anything and everything to try to bring them down.

All of us are in charge of something. Some of us are in charge of large corporations or agencies. Others are in charge of our children, our future. Some of us are not in charge of anything more than ourselves. But that's good news. To simply be in charge of our own thinking is an elevation. There are a great many people who seem incapable of producing their own thoughts or opinions. Being in charge of millions does not matter if the person is not in charge of his or her own joy, peace, and happiness. Shadrach, Meshach, and Abednego were not only in charge of the affairs of Babylon; they were in charge of their own beliefs, choices, and actions.

When Nebuchadnezzar heard the news he flew into a rage. He was unbalanced. He was furious because all the various nations, languages, and cultures were bowing down at the appropriate time, but the Jews were not. This powerful ruler of multitudes let the actions of three young men determine his behavior. He was stuck on stupid. Everyone was bowing except Shadrach, Meshach, and Abednego, so the king decided to make an example of them. He decided to throw them into a furnace hot enough to burn even the soldiers who led them to the entrance!

The three did not try to defend themselves against the king's accusation. At that point, the battle was not between the three Hebrews and the Babylonian king. The battle was between God and His opposers. In verse 17, the three uttered some of the most powerful faith words in the Bible: "The God we serve is able to save us from it, and he will rescue us from your hand, O king. But even if he does not, we want you to know, O king, that we will not serve your gods or worship the image of gold you have set up."

God is Jehovah-Jireh—a God who is able to provide. God is Jehovah Ra-ah—our Shepherd. God is able to stand, heal, and deliver. So many of us have given the Lord conditions. We will serve the Lord as long as our own terms are met. But the Lord wants us to bless Him, love Him, and follow Him even if He doesn't do what we want. Even if He doesn't rescue us from the heat, He wants us to bless Him anyway. Anybody can bless the Lord when everything is going well. But it takes real faith to bless the Lord when everything is going wrong.

In verses 19-21, Nebuchadnezzar lost his temper, and his face turned red with anger against Shadrach, Meshach, and Abednego. He ordered the furnace to be heated up seven times hotter than normal. He commanded the strongest men in his army to tie the three men up and throw them into the blazing furnace. In order to further induce heat, they tied them up fully dressed so that their clothing would burn.

The flames were so hot that they consumed the guards who escorted the men to the furnace. But when Shadrach, Meshach, and Abednego—who were bound and fully clothed—fell into the blazing fire, Nebuchadnezzar leaped to his feet in amazement. He asked his officials, "Didn't we tie up three men?" They responded, "Yes, we did Your Majesty." His sense of reality confirmed, Nebuchadnezzar said in verse 25, "Look! I see four men walking around in the fire, unbound and unharmed, and the fourth looks like a son of the gods." The three Hebrews went into the fire bound up, but when the king saw them with the Son of God, they were walking around unbound and unharmed. We can be in the heat and the ropes burn; yet everything else stays intact. The text says that none of their hair was singed. No smoke was in their clothing. They had no blisters. But the fire did burn the ropes, and they were able to walk around in the fire.

We can be in the heat and the ropes burn; yet everything else stays intact.

If God does not keep us from the fire, then God will keep us in the fire until He delivers us out of the fire. Sometimes God will let us go through the fire to get beyond some things that had us bound. He will let us go into the fire. Impossible? No. Every day we can see an example of men and women who stand in the fire and beat the heat. People watch strong believers and wonder how we can stand the heat of our persecutions. They wonder how we can walk around unharmed in the midst of fire. Strong believers can be compared to a microwave oven. When popcorn is cooked in a microwave, the popcorn get hot enough to pop, but the paper bag containing it does not burn. Bacon cooked in the microwave gets done, but it does not burn the paper wrapped around it. Sometimes, I believe, God lets us go into the fire because certain people, bad habits, bad attitudes, or bad thinking need to be burned out of our lives. When we are in the heat we need to pray, "Lord, I don't know why I'm in this heat, but I thank You that I haven't burned up. I thank You that You are keeping me in the midst of this flame. I don't like being in this heat, but I know You are doing something in me, with me, and through me while I'm in the heat."

The Jesus of the New Testament had showed up in the heat of the Old Testament.

At the sight of the men walking in the flames unharmed, King Nebuchadnezzar had a theophany: "Wait a minute! We put in three, but now there are four. And one of them looks like a son of the gods." The Jesus of the New Testament had showed up in the heat of the Old Testament. When Israel was going to Canaan, He showed up as a pillar of fire at night. When Moses was on the back side of the mountain, Jesus got his attention in a burning bush and said, "Take off your shoes for the ground upon which you stand is holy ground." Jesus was there in the fire with Shadrach, Meshach, and Abednego. And He will be there in the fire with us. He will keep us in perfect peace if we keep our minds stayed on Him.

Nebuchadnezzar told Shadrach, Meshach, and Abednego to come out. He now recognized them as "servants of the Most High God." The three came out, stepping over the bones of the men who had thrown them in. When we wait on the Lord, we will meet again with those who brought upon us the heat of persecution. Only when we meet up with them again, we will be exalted, victorious. But while Shadrach, Meshach, and Abednego came out, the fourth one, the Son of God, did not. He remained in the furnace. Jesus stands waiting in the furnace, just in case we get thrown in.

Anybody can stand with God as long as things are going well. Such persons can dance as long as there is money in their pockets. Anybody can dance because a spouse is being loving and kind. Anybody can dance while moving up the corporate ladder. But when a person gets thrown into the fire, the question is, will that person stand with God? Shadrach, Meshach, and Abednego were willing to stand with the Lord even in the fire. They stood with the Lord even when they had a chance to back out and denounce the God of Abraham, Isaac, and Jacob. They were willing to go into the fire because they knew that their God would be in there with them. That out-of-balance golden god could not go into the fire, but the God who delivered Israel from Egypt could and would deliver them as well.

Their experience with persecution has yielded for all generations the ultimate faith statement: "We know that the God we serve is able to deliver us from the fire. But even if he does not, we will not bow to your god." Shadrach, Meshach, and Abednego knew that being in the fire with the true God was better than being outside the fire with a fake, out-of-balance god.

Since they could not get him to Jesus because of the crowd, they made an opening in the roof above Jesus and, after digging through it, lowered the mat the paralyzed man was lying on. When Jesus saw their faith, he said to the paralytic, "Son, your sins are forgiven."

Mark 2:4-5, NIV

IMAGINATION

Mark 2:1-12

Going forward and acting on his faith in Jesus Christ, the paralytic, employed his imagination to gain healing and wholeness from the Master.

I magine if are two of the most powerful words in the world. When imagination is operative, neurons in the human brain are deployed that unleash forces that can change our lives and transform our world.

Every invention is the result of someone's imagination. Henry Ford imagined the automobile, and the Model T was born. Bill Gates imagined wide access to home computers, and now millions of people around the world are cruising on the information superhighway. Dr. Martin Luther King Jr. imagined a world of equal rights for people of color, and today we have civil rights legislation in America. Henry T. Sampson imagined the cellular telephone and received a patent on July 6, 1971. Today, most people in the United States have at least one. Black people are credited with inventing many laborsaving devices, perhaps because our people were the ones doing all of the labor! And as we worked, we imagined a way to make the work easier.

Disney World in Orlando, Florida is 40 miles larger than the city of Manhattan. Disney World was dedicated in 1971. Walt Disney, founder of the Disney empire, died several years before the dedication. Someone said to his wife, "If only Walt were here to see this." Her response was, "He did see it, and that's why we are here." Walt Disney imagined the mega theme park before it became a reality.

Eddie Kendricks, an original member of the Temptations, sang about a woman that he wanted to marry, have children with, and share a house with in the country. Every time he looked at her he thought about how lucky he was. There was only one hitch—she wasn't his woman, except in his imagination. All he had was a picture. He saw it before it became a reality. That's important because he had to see that woman in his imagination before he could have her.

Imagination is the picture-making power of the human brain that allows us to form mental images not present or never before wholly actualized. One of the characteristics of faith is an activated imagination.

Albert Einstein, a brilliant scientist understood the power of imagination. He said, "Imagination is more important than knowledge." Muhammad Ali said, "The man who has no imagination has no wings." George Bernard Shaw said, "You see things and you say, 'Why?' But I dream things that never were and say, 'Why not?'"

Einstein also observed that, "Your imagination is your preview of life's coming attractions." When we go to the movies, before the featured attraction plays we view coming attractions. And in our believer's imagination, we should have a preview of coming attractions— coming attractions for the fall, coming attractions for the winter, for next year.

"If the winds of fortune are temporarily blowing against you, remember that you can harness them and make them carry you toward your definite purpose, through the use of your imagination."

— Napoleon Hill

Imagination is a powerful force that God wants His creation to activate. God wants believers to activate our imaginations because we are in an imagination war with the forces of evil. Imagination can be a powerful force for evil as well as good. Adolph Hitler had a wickedly vivid imagination. He imagined a world without Jews, and the Holocaust was born. Timothy McVeigh imagined that he was at war against our government, and over 100 men, women, and children were killed in the Edward R. Murrow Federal Building in Oklahoma City. The "Trenchcoat Mafia" of Columbine High School imagined their bloody revenge against certain members of the student body. Two young men activated their imaginations to do wickedness because of a crazy songwriter named Marilyn Manson.

One reason it is important for believers to activate imagination is because we are being out-imagined by unbelievers. Too many young black males can imagine a life only of gang banging and prison bars. Too many young black females can imagine only a life of early motherhood and relating to men as "my baby daddy," not "my husband." Hitler had imagination. McVeigh had it. The Trenchcoat Mafia had it. Every nut, fruit, and flake who ever did an evil deed had imagination. Yet, many of us who are saved, Holy Spirit-filled, and Bible-directed are being out-imagined by the world. It doesn't make sense. If someone builds a massive gambling casino, it's called imagination. But if a church gives sacrificially to build a nice facility where families can pray and play together, people want to call it a cult. It seems that it is acceptable to use our imagination for sin, but we cannot use our imagination for God. Ephesians 3:20 affirms that our Lord "is able to do immeasurably more than all we ask or imagine, according to his power that is at work within us."

One reason it is important for believers to activate imagination is because we are being out-imagined by unbelievers.

A second reason God wants us to activate our imaginations is that it is through our imagination that God gets things done. Many of our social and personal problems are solved through activated imaginations. God does not waste miracles. God does not do for us what He has given us the imagination to do for ourselves.

The story goes that George Washington Carver asked God to tell him what is in the peanut. God told him, "You have an imagination. Go find out for yourself." Because Carver used his imagination, he devised more uses for the peanut than had ever been created. He imagined paste, paint, glue—300 household products from the peanut.

A second reason God wants us to activate our imaginations is that it is through our imagination that God gets things done.

To illustrate the power of faithful imagination, look at this story in Mark's Gospel. Jesus is in the house teaching and the people are gathered in and around the house to listen to Him. We can imagine many things for our church house or our own house, but if Jesus is not in the house, whatever is going on inside cannot yield a positive result.

In Mark 2:1, the news had spread that Jesus was in the house. What a wonderful rumor! One of the persons who heard the rumor was a paralyzed man. He was anxious to get to Jesus. Four times in the story he is called paralyzed (vss. 3,5,9,10). The frequent references to his condition mean that he was totally incapacitated and incapable of movement under his own volition—like Christopher Reeves or Joni Erickson Tada, who once said that she was so helpless she could not even commit suicide.

Inspiration Leads to Imagination

Although the paralyzed man was confined to a mat, he somehow had gotten the news that Jesus was teaching in a nearby house. Knowing that Jesus is in the house is always inspirational. Quite possibly, the man had heard about Jesus and His healing power. He may have heard that Jesus had healed lepers, the lame, the blind, and the deaf, or that He had walked on water. That the man got inspired on his mat helps us to know that we can be inspired even when we are down on our backs. It is possible to have a view of coming attractions even while laid out on a mat. The man saw a coming attraction of himself walking the streets like other men. He was inspired by the thought of using a mat only for sleeping and not for living. Having heard about Jesus' reputation, the paralytic was moved from inspiration to investigation. He got four friends to help him get to Jesus. He wanted to find out for himself what this man from Nazareth could do.

The paralytic could not rely on his own dormant limbs in order to go and find out if the rumors about Jesus were true. What he could depend on was his active imagination. He enlisted the help of four men to carry him to the house where Jesus was teaching. When they got there they couldn't get in because of the crowd. Undaunted, they went to the front door, then to the back door, and around to the window, but they couldn't get in. Refusing to be denied access to Jesus, they went up on top of the house, made a hole in the roof, and lowered the man to Jesus. When Jesus saw their faith, he said to the paralytic, "Son, your sins are forgiven."

The house most likely had the common external stairway leading to a flat roof. The construction of the roof probably was of poles across the space between the walls, with smaller sticks and reeds forming a network across the poles. This material was covered with some kind of matting and hardened earth or mud.

There were many people gathered there to hear Jesus that day. Many others probably wanted to be healed, just like the paralytic. But

Mark records only one healing at the house. Why was this man the only one healed that day? There are a number of possibilities that may explain why this man was healed and others were not. Generally, human beings are inspired by one of three conditions: we have enough, we know enough, or we hurt enough. Apparently, the paralytic had grown weary of his confinement. The man's healing began with his inspiration. The word spirit is contained within the word inspiration. The man's body was incapacitated, but his spirit of hope was quite active. The man did not simply lie on his mat believing that paralysis was his destiny.

The man did not simply lie on his mat believing that paralysis was his destiny.

Investigation Leads to Imagination

The man went from inspiration to investigation. It is not enough to be inspired if we do not go and investigate. The paralytic got four friends to carry him to the house where Jesus was teaching. He probably enlisted one friend for each corner of the mat. Holding up one corner of his mat was Freddy Faith. Another corner was supported by his friend Harry Hope. The third corner was balanced by Larry Love. And on the fourth corner was Danny Determination. We all need faith, hope, love, and determination to see us through life's challenges.

Probably the most imaginative person of the 20th century was Thomas Edison, who has over 1,000 patents to his credit. But when someone referred to him as a genius, he told the person that of the 1,000 inventions, only one was his originally...and that was the phonograph. Edison said that all of his other inventions were picked up from other people's abandoned ideas. Edison must have looked at these abandoned ideas and then investigated further. Upon investigation and determination that the idea was a good one, he disciplined it, developed it, and deployed it.

Our imaginations must be kept active and working because we can be inspired at any moment. Imagination can be fueled in the most unlikely of places. For example, the common practice of using anesthesia for surgery was not developed in a laboratory, or even in a hospital, as one might think. The idea was spawned in church. A physician was listening to a sermon about God putting Adam to sleep to perform the surgery to remove his rib. The physician thought, "Wouldn't that be interesting?" His imagination was fueled and he investigated the concept further.

Irritation Fuels Imagination

After being fueled with inspiration and investigation, the paralytic and his four friends experienced irritation. When they got to the house, the house was crowded and they could not get to Jesus. Many things can block us from getting to Jesus. In fact, that is Satan's job. It can be people, places, things, or thoughts. Is anything blocking you from getting to Jesus?

For the paralytic and his friends, the crowd was in the way. There was the Front Door Committee who blocked their entrance because they deemed it their responsibility to determine who could enter through the front door and when. The committee probably

Many things can block us from getting to Jesus. In fact, that is Satan's job. It can be people, places, things, or thoughts.

looked at the paralytic and company, determined them to be nobodies, and denied them access. So they decided to try the Back Door Committee, who, after getting a tip off from the Front Door Committee, told the men, "Not this way." The Window Committee said their entrance in this manner was unorthodox and therefore could not be done; entrance to the house could come only through the door.

Those who have childlike faith are better able to activate faithful imagination in putting God's Word into action.

Having experienced all of these barriers, they could have gone home or waited, as we say, for a breakthrough. But faith doesn't wait for a breakthrough. Faith makes its own breakthrough. Faith makes its own breakthrough by activating imagination. The men went from inspiration to investigation to irritation. All the doors and windows were shut. All of the traditional methods were closed to them. Perhaps the man was willing to give up but his friends told him, "No, Man. You made us carry you all this way. We ain't leaving here until you see Jesus." They may have been men who didn't understand all of the particulars of social or religious protocol. All they knew was their friend needed to be healed, and if it was ever going to happen the Man inside named Jesus was the only one who could do it.

Once the men experienced irritation at being denied access after coming all this way, the only recourse left for them if there was to be a change in the paralytic's condition was imagination. We don't have to pray for imagination. We are born with it. Children have it in abundance. The psychology behind child's play is imagination. Give a little girl a doll and in her imagination, she's a mother. Give a little boy a basketball and in his imagination, he's

Kobe Bryant. No adult can rival the imagination of a child. Perhaps that is why Jesus prayed, "I praise you, Father, Lord of heaven and earth, because you have hidden these things from the wise and learned, and revealed them to little children" (Matthew 11:25). Those who have childlike faith are better able to activate faithful imagination in putting God's Word into action.

When we grow up, we tend to bury our imagination because of negative conditioning. We get out of touch with our imaginative gifts because of imagination blockers. For example, the first imagination blocker is low self-image. A person with a low self-image says, "I don't activate my imagination because I don't believe I have any." Husbands don't romance their wives because they think they have no imagination. Youth may not aspire to do more academically because they think they have no imagination. We can know that we have imagination because we all were made in the image of God. Part of God's image is creativity. His creativity is displayed in every aspect of nature . . .in seasons and how they change, in flowers and the animal kingdom —from the aardvark to the zebra. And because we are made in His image, we too are creative. When we dress up, that's imagination. We are imaginative in our dress, in our speech, and in the way we express ourselves. There is nothing more imaginative than a black woman's hairdo. A black woman can have an updo, finger waves, and braids all in the same hairdo!

The second imagination blocker is habit. The story of the pike and the minnows may be familiar to you. In an aquarium lived a large pike. One day a transparent plate of glass was put in the tank separating one side from the other. On the opposite side from the pike, the experimenter put in several minnows. When the pike saw the minnows, he went after them, but was inhibited by the glass wall. The plate of glass separated the pike from the minnows for about a month. After that, the glass was removed, but the pike no longer tried to catch the minnows. He no longer believed he could. His habit was established through the presence of the glass wall.

Habit says there is only one right way to do something. So in this story, habit and tradition said that to get into a building you must enter through the door. Imagination says I will break with tradition and habit and go through the roof.

All creative persons are simply people who refuse to allow people to put them in a box. As Howard Hendrix put it, "They color outside the lines." When Walt Disney was a kid, he painted faces on his flowers. His teacher told him that flowers don't have faces. He responded, "Mine do." He would have lost his imagination if he had allowed his teacher to define for him what is possible. Just think, had Walt Disney believed the comments of just one imagination blocker, we might never have had The Wonderful World of Disney, Disneyland, Disney World, Mickey Mouse & Co., and the all the rest that is Disney.

The paralytic and his friends were successful because they imagined going through the roof. Great achievements start with imagination, like Harriett Tubman or Mary McLeod Bethune, or the contributions of great inventors. When the telephone was first thought of someone almost got arrested. In 1865, eleven years before Alexander Graham Bell's patent, an American named Joshua Coopersmith was arrested when he tried to raise money to build a telephone system. After the arrest, a strident Boston Post editorial cried: Well-informed people know it is impossible to transmit the voice over wires and that were it possible to do so the thing would be of no practical value. In 1899, there was a law attempted to close the U.S. Patent Office. The head of the patent office believed that everything that could be invented had been invented already.

Many kids today cannot determine what they will be doing when they grow up because many of the jobs that employ people today were not in existence 10 years ago. Today's church is not like the early church. Today we have jumbotrons—huge viewing monitors—so that thousands of people can see the speaker up close. We have sermons aided by PowerPoint™ presentations. We have tithe and offering payments through automatic bank withdrawals. There are laptop ports in the pews. Some families may say, "We only go through the door." Because of habit and tradition they may limit their opportunities for growth and intimacy as a family.

The third imagination blocker is fear—fear of mistakes, fear of being criticized, fear of being labeled, of being considered eccentric, of the opinions of others. Fear blocks the possibility for faithful imagination, which yields positive results, and fuels negative imagination, which yields disaster. Faithful imagination moves us forward. Negative imagination moves us backward. God's Word is an imagination builder: "I can do everything through him who gives me strength" (Philippians 4:13).

While Jesus was teaching, there was a noise on the roof. Dust was flying, pieces of roof were falling on the heads of sleeping deacons. He was moved by their imagination, fueled by their faith. When you have faith you can, like the old school group Parliament Funkadelic sang, "Tear the Roof off the Sucka." After the man was healed, instead of marveling and glorifying God, all that the religious leaders could do was criticize Jesus. But the Master, knowing their thoughts, asked, "What is easier...?" Many people today turn their noses up at imagination and innovation when employed in ministry. As soon as somebody's church starts growing or a new ministry

Many people today turn their noses up at imagination and innovation when employed in ministry.

grows in popularity, the religious traditionalists begin to criticize instead of praising God that more people are being reached for the Kingdom.

What healed the paralytic was imagination. The true test of spiritual imagination is Does the idea glorify God? Our imagination should move us in directions that give all praise and glory to God. Where does your imagination lead you? Do you imagine ways to lead people to Jesus? Do you imagine ways to give glory and honor to God? Or do you imagine ways that serve no purpose other than to line your own pockets? Does your imagination take you to thoughts of revenge or retaliation against someone you feel has done you wrong?

Our imagination should move us in directions that give all praise and glory to God.

Verse 12 says that when the people saw what Jesus had done for the paralyzed man, they praised God. If you want to see some things in your life that you have never seen before, if you want to see yourself rise to new levels, if you want to see yourself doing things that other people said could not be done, activate your imagination through your faith in God.

Many people throughout the Scriptures, responded "It Was Just My [Holy Ghost] Imagination..."

• After Moses had led his people out of Egypt, he could say "It Was Just My [Holy Ghost] Imagination..."

• After the ark Noah built was sustaining him, his family, and representatives of the entire animal kingdom atop the floodwaters, he could say, "It Was Just My [Holy Ghost] Imagination..."

- After Deborah's victory over Sisera and his army and Jael's plan for the demise of Sisera inside her tent, she could say "It Was Just My [Holy Ghost] Imagination..."

- After Joshua's victory battle at Jericho he could say "It Was Just My [Holy Ghost] Imagination..."

- Following the revelation for Gideon's strategy for victory over the Midianites he could say "It Was Just My [Holy Ghost] Imagination..."

- After Mary gave birth to this special child through Immaculate Conception, she could say "It Was Just My [Holy Ghost] Imagination..."

- Following Peter's miraculous release from prison, he could say "It Was Just My [Holy Ghost] Imagination..."

In Eddie Kendricks' mind, he was living a happy and fulfilled life with the woman he loved. After a while, however, he realized it was only his imagination. But faithful imagination, instead of leading to hurt and disillusionment, leads to Kingdom results. God's people can activate their divinely inspired imagination to bring forth the impossible.

"Lord, if it's you," Peter replied, *"tell me to come to you on the water."*

Matthew 14:28, NIV

Adventure

Matthew 14:25-32

*As Peter grew in discipleship and faith in his Teacher, Peter experienced
adventure with the Master, the likes of which no other person has known.*

Benjamin E. Mays, the late great educator and president emeritus of Morehouse College would challenge the men of Morehouse by reminding them that there is no house like Morehouse. For at Morehouse, he said, "We do not put crowns on the heads of our men. But we put crowns far above the heads of our men and bid them to grow tall enough to wear it." Dr. Mays was fond of quoting a poem of unknown origin that says:

I don't want my boat to remain
Far inside the harbor bar.
I want to go out in the deep
Out where the big ships are.
And if my little ship,
Should prove too light.
For the billows that sweep o'er
I would rather go down in the stirring fight.
Than to droves to death by the sheltered shore.

This poem reflects two philosophies of life. One that says, "I want to remain by the sheltered shore. I don't want to take any risks." The other says, "I want to go out in the stirring waters. I'd rather go down doing something significant, than to live doing something insignificant and succeed at it."

It is better to attempt to do something significant for God and fail, than to do nothing and succeed. Life is supposed to be an adventure. Usually when we think about our relationship to God, we think of Him as our Protector and our defense. The old folks sang, "Jesus, be a fence all around me. Protect me as I travel along the way." Those images of God are accurate. He is our defense and our fence—our fortress, our strong tower. The philosophy of Job teaches that God has a hedge all around us. Many troubles we do not encounter because God has placed a hedge of protection around us.

But that's not the only image we should have of God. He not only keeps us safe, but He places us in less-than-safe situations. He wants us to venture and step out on a limb. If you're afraid to step out on a limb, you'll never get the fruit. The fruit is out on the limb! He didn't keep David safe. David faced Goliath—that was an adventure. Shadrach, Meshach, and Abednego were not kept from facing danger. Their defiance of Nebuchadnezzar became an adventure. The expansion of the church in Acts was a adventure. Paul went through Asia Minor and the Mediterranean world was an adventure. And God has an adventure for the church. He has an adventure for every life. God does not want us to be couch potatoes! Get off the couch! Get out of the boat!

Mark Buchanan has written a book entitled, *Your God Is Too Safe* (Multnomah Publishers, 2001). He asserts that God is the One in whom we find refuge. He is our hiding place, a shield about us....our Ace in the Hole.

This produces a safe God. And these characteristics are true...He is our refuge, strength, hiding place, etc. But God is also calling us as Christians to a life of adventure...to engage in something daring. The Christian faith is more than intellectual assent to a set of doctrinal positions. Christianity, at its best, is a call to a great adventure; for example, repentance, forgiveness, loving one's enemy, world evangelization was a great adventure.

Peter's walking on the water is an example of a great adventure. There are those who would seek to dismiss the miraculous in this text. There are many pseudo scholars or pseudo intellectuals who would try to make us believe that Peter really didn't walk on water. They dismiss it as myth, fable, or allegory. They have an "anti-supernatural" bias. At the turn of the 20th century, Rudolph Bultmann did what he termed the demythologizing of Scripture. His philosophy says that any time we come across a miraculous event, you have to demythologize it to make the story more palatable. Bible scholars like Bultmann seek to explain away the miraculous events of the Bible.

Other Bible scholars have postulated that the disciples were disoriented in the storm that night. Their emotional discombobulation caused them to see things that are not really so. Imagine that Jesus was walking on the water, and that He was, in fact, standing on the shore. When Peter said, "Bid me to come to you on the water." Jesus said, "Come." Peter stepped out of the boat and tripped. He fell out into the water and thought he was drowning. Jesus picked him up, ridiculed Peter for his lack of faith, got in the boat, and they sailed on across.

The same holds true for the story of the feeding of the 5,000. Some have attempted to explain away the banquet in the wilderness so that it fits within the human context of understanding. Their theory is that the magnanimous

There are many pseudo scholars or pseudo intellectuals who would try to make us believe that Peter really didn't walk on water.

spirit of the little boy who pulled out his lunch shamed the others into bringing out the food they had been hiding for themselves. As a result, there was enough to feed everyone. The problem with this explanation is that it removes the miraculous and brings in the rational.

But the God we serve is not rational from the human perspective of rationality. He is, however, supernatural. I believe in a miracle-working, wonder-working God who can do for us what we can never do for ourselves. I believe that Jesus walked on water. And I believe that He enabled Peter to walk on water. Moreover, I believe that He wants every disciple to become a water-walker.

An atheistic teacher was arguing to a Christian kid that it was impossible for Peter to walk on the water because of the laws of gravity. The Christian student insisted that it did happen. The kid said, "When I get to heaven, I'm going to ask Peter did he really walk on water."

The teacher says, "Well suppose Peter went to hell."

"Well then, you can ask him," the boy replied.

I believe that Peter really and truly walked on water. It harmonizes with God's pattern of calling us into a life of adventure. It was a busy day in their lives. Jesus had been teaching all day. He had fed the 5,000-plus. The crowd tried to nominate Jesus as their King by acclamation. Jesus did not want His disciples seduced by such accolades. John 6:15 reveals that Jesus, knew that they intended to come and make Him king by force. To circumvent this, He withdrew again to a mountain by himself.

Jesus compelled His disciples to get into the boat, which means he forced them. The word compelled is a strong term. It suggests that Peter and the disciples liked the attention of the crowds. The liked the adulation. In other words, they were star struck. They were reluctant to leave the fawning of thousands. In fact, it just may have been their finest hour. They were basking in the glow of their newfound popularity. They felt as though they were hot commodities. No doubt, they had visions of livin' large that included book deals, movie rights, autograph sessions, product endorsements, talk show circuits, and maybe even political office. James and John, the sons of Zebedee revealed their aspirations for power (Mark 10:35-44).

Jesus had to compel them to get into the boat before they could sign their first book deal, negotiate their first movie contract, or move on to fame and glory. Jesus did not want His disciples to get "caught up" in a whirlwind of worldliness.

One of the reasons why deer get killed is because deer are drawn to bright glare of headlights. Bug Zapper® works because what draws bugs to the light is the very thing that kills them—the light. The world has some powerful draws that can kill you. Crack can draw you with the promise of euphoria, but it can kill you. You can be drawn to every fine sista or brotha who comes on to you, but it could kill you. You can be drawn to the Super Value menu at Wendy's, but it could kill you. Some preachers let the limelight kill their ministry. They become more interested in selfish fulfillment than service to Christ. Some students let the light of partying and popularity draw them away from getting a degree.

Jesus told them to cross on the other side of the Sea of Galilee, which was about seven miles, while He went into the mountains to pray. This was in the evening. But that night something went terribly wrong. And things do go wrong as we cross the sea of life. Off the slopes of Mt. Hermon the powerful winds lashed the

Jesus did not want His disciples to get "caught up" in a whirlwind of worldliness.

water into a fury. It tossed that little boat the disciples were in like a juggler juggles a ball. Their little boat was battered by the waves. It was so tormenting and so violent that their concern was not making to the other side, but merely staying alive.

Here is a lesson to learn from this: Obedience to Christ is no guarantee that believers will be spared adversity. The disciples encountered the storm because they had obeyed Christ. He is the one who told them to get into the boat. Did Jesus know in advance that He was sending them into a storm? I think we have to allow it. Because if our meteorologists can come on television and tell us weather patterns a week in advance, surely Christ knew that He was sending His disciples into a storm. Why did He do it? Because there are some life lessons that we learn only while we are in the midst of a storm. The poet wrote:

Obedience to Christ is no guarantee that believers will be spared adversity.

> I walked a mile with pleasure.
> She chatted all the way.
> But left me none the better,
> For all she had to say.
> I walked a mile with Sorrow,
> And not a word said she.
> But oh, the things I learned,
> When Sorrow walked with me.

We often say that the stars come out at night. But the fact is that the stars are always out, even in the daylight. But you cannot see the stars until it is night. We will not experience certain things until it is dark in our lives. Perhaps is has to be dark to get our attention. The activity and busyness that occurs in the light can distract us from

God. The text says that at three o'clock, Jesus came to them walking on the water.

This was not the first time the disciples had been in a storm with Jesus. If you follow Jesus, you are going to experience a few storms in life. They had been in a storm earlier, but Jesus was on the boat with them. This storm occurred at night. That storm was during the day. In that storm Jesus said, "Peace, be still" and the winds and the waves obeyed Him. The disciples were fearful, but Jesus was faithful. Those are always the two responses to life's storms—fear or faith. Either you will have peace or you will have petulance. When Jesus calmed the seas, the disciples wondered, "What manner of man is this?"

Jesus did not calm this second storm. In this storm, no such command was given. Could it be that Jesus was preparing His disciples for the time when His physical presence would not be in the boat? But even when His presence is not there, He is watching us, monitoring our movements. It is always more important that God see us than that we see God. If we are in a storm, and He wants us to move from a stormy situation, He will give us a hiding place. If He doesn't move us from the storm, He will give us grace. God will either give you the place or the grace. But through it all, He will keep us.

This storm on the Sea of Galilee they encountered because Jesus told them to get on the boat. They encountered a storm because they obeyed Jesus. He knew the storm was coming, but He still told them to get on the boat. I believe He knew because if meteorologists, with all of their scientific instruments, can forecast a storm, surely God Incarnate can do so. He knows when our storms are coming, but we don't know. Being omnipotent, He could have warned them about the storm. He could have cautioned them to stay behind until the storm was over. But He didn't do that. He will let His disciples go through a storm because, although we don't like storms, we learn more about

Him by going through storms than through sunshine. Our faith is developed strengthened through the storms of life. Our testimony comes from the storm. A lot of people want to testi-lie. But if you want to testify, you have to go through some storms. Just because you are encountering a storm doesn't mean you are outside of God's will. We've got this pop, New Age theology that says, "If I'm a Christian and live on a certain spiritual plain, I will not experience any storms." But all of us are either in a storm, just coming out of a storm, or on our way to a storm. No disciple is exempt from storms.

No matter how long we have been on our Christian walk, we will experience storms. The disciples were experienced men of the sea, not neophytes, but they could not avoid the storm. They made their living on the sea. So, if these professional seamen were frightened, this was a serious storm. It was like nothing they had encountered and Jesus seemed absent. He was nowhere to be found. During the other storm, He was in the boat with them. It's easy to go through a storm when we know Jesus is with us. But when we feel like He has abandoned us, the storms get hard.

Everything was in the boat with them but Jesus. There was fish, water, confusion, fear, and anxiety in the boat, but no Jesus. Where is Jesus? Time passes, and still no Jesus. Sometimes we have protracted storms, like El Niño. Some have been in a storm for a long time, and have been praying and doing their best, and they wonder, "Where is Jesus?" I maintain it's none of our business where Jesus is. We don't need to know where He is. But we can take comfort in knowing He is always where He's supposed to be. More important, it's not necessary to know where Jesus is. It's all important that Jesus know where we are. Even when we can't trace Him, we can trust Him.

When the disciples encountered this storm it was night. When they first saw Christ, they thought they had seen a ghost. Thought they had died and gone to the world of departed spirits. Jesus said, "Fear not." Peter saw this as an opportunity for the walk of adventure. He said, "If that be thee, bid me to come to you out on the water." And Jesus said, "Come."

Notice Peter did not ask for any guarantees. That is the very meaning of adventure—there are no guarantees. He also did not ask for any explanations. He didn't ask how he was going to do walk on water. More importantly, before Peter struck out on an adventure he first got permission. He asked for no guarantees, only for an opportunity for adventure. This was not a foolish impulse on Peter's part. It was not a daredevil instinct he needed to fulfill. This was not bungee jumping, or tornado chasing in a Pinto, or risk-taking for the sake of a thrill. He wanted to get close to Jesus, even if it meant getting in the middle of a storm. This was extreme discipleship. Sometimes the only way we can get close to Him and experience that extreme discipleship is to move deeper into the storm.

Sometimes the only way we can get close to Him and experience that extreme discipleship is to move deeper into the storm.

Peter wanted to take a walk of adventure with Jesus. Jesus' response to Peter's extreme discipleship was, "Come," and Peter was walking on water. How did He do it? How did Jesus perform a miracle. My late grandfather, the Reverend Dr. B. J. Miller explained it to me this way. The law of gravity is a law, but it becomes nullified when a greater law transcends it. For example, if a pen drops from my hand, it will fall to the ground because the magnetic force of gravity draws everything to itself. However, if I am able to catch the pen by putting my hand between the pen and the floor, it will not fall. That is because something stronger and greater was placed between the falling pen and its gravitational pull. The law of gravity has remained in tact; however, it was nullified by a stronger, greater force.

If Peter had stepped on the water without permission, he would have been guilty of presumptuousness. That is a lesson to us: We should never venture without divine permission, whether in jobs, marriage, etc. Don't get out of the boat until God says "Come." But when Jesus said, "Come" had Peter remained in the boat, he would have been guilty of the sin of disobedience.

Notice that all Jesus said was "Come." Jesus gave no guarantees or explanations. This was not calm water. The water is turbulent and the wind was at gale force. But Jesus said "Come." He did not say, "Come when the wind dies down." He did not say, "Come when the water is calm." He did not say "Come after everything has been figured out." But He said, "Come."

Many people are waiting for the ideal time to do something adventurous. But if you're waiting until everything settles down, until there are no more problems, until everyone understands you, then you will never experience adventure because there will always be problems. There will always be a reason not to do something adventurous. That's the excuse of the person who is waiting for the right time to tithe, the right time to go back to school, the right time to answer God's call, or the right time to commit to Jesus. Anyone waiting for the right time will have to stay in the boat.

When Peter stepped out of the boat, he was not stepping on the water. He was stepping on a promise. As R. Kelso Carter wrote in his "Standing on the Promises," Peter was standing on the promises of God—the promises that cannot fail.

His promise is not that we will live free of trouble or strive. God never promised a trouble-free life. But as the saying goes, "God won't take you where His grace won't keep you." If He takes you to the lion's den, He'll keep you. Ask Daniel. If He takes you to a fiery furnace, He'll keep you. Ask Shadrach, Meshach, and Abednego. If He allows you to stand before a giant warrior, He'll give you victory. Ask David.

Peter began to walk when he looked at Jesus. When we keep our eyes fixed on Jesus, He'll keep us in perfect peace. But then Peter thought about what he was doing, wondering how the impossible was made possible, he took his mind off Jesus and became problem-focused, not Christ-focused. But when he began to fall, he knew what to do. He didn't wait until he was all the way under. As soon as he began to sink he cried out, "Lord, save me!" He didn't call on the other men in the boat. There was no time for a long prayer. A long prayer is not always necessary. He will hear the prayer and answer.

After they came through the storm, they worshiped Him. But I believe Peter worshiped differently than the other disciples because of what he had been through. He had been in the midst of the storm with Jesus. When we go through the storms of life and Jesus brings us out, we have something to shout about. We worship differently, in a way that others may not understand. Simon the Pharisee did not understand why the woman came to his house and worshiped Jesus by anointing His feet with tears and wiping them clean with her hair (Luke 7:36-50). Jesus explained her act of worship this way: "She loves much because she has been forgiven much." Likewise, when we have experienced much and Christ has brought us out, our faith response is more significant.

When we keep our eyes fixed on Jesus, He'll keep us in perfect peace.

Two decades of pastoral experience have taught me that everybody has a boat. A person's boat is what that person finds security in apart from God. A person's boat may be a relationship he need to get out of, but it gives him some sense of security. A person's boat may be her vocation, which she thinks is her security. A person's boat may be trying to please parents in anticipation of an inheritance that is presumed to offer security. Like the rich young ruler in the Gospels, a boat may be a person's bank account. Like Nicodemus, a person's boat may be social standing. Hanging on to the boat can cause a believer to miss out on a spiritual adventure.

Peter was willing to leave the boat and walk out on faith. After he got out there, what kept Peter from sinking was the promise of Christ. That word "come" is more powerful than gravity. The text reveals that Peter was doing fine, but when he saw the wind, when he looked away from Christ, he became self-aware. He took his eyes off of the promise and began to sink. What brought Peter down was not the water, but the worry. What brings disciples down is not the storm itself, but the worry we engage in over the storm. When Peter began to worry about the wind and the water he began to sink. His worrying became like rocks in Peter's pocket.

With all of the troubles that our people face, most of us should be under the water. African Americans have lived in stormy conditions that should have taken us under. But through our faith in God we have remained buoyant. Peter regained his buoyancy because he did a wonderful thing when he was just beginning to sink. His actions tell us when and how to call on the Lord. The time to call on God is not after we've already gone under. God wants to be our first recourse, not our last option. Peter didn't pray a long plea. He didn't engage in a long theological discourse. He cried, "Lord, save me!", much like the thief on the cross. He didn't go into all of that "Lord, I'm coming to You with bowed head, humble heart, and on bended knee...."

The question is Who's the failure in this story? It was not Peter, but those who remained in the boat. His experience on the water yielded many great discoveries for the disciple. Peter discovered the exhilaration of water walking as directed by the Savior. He also discovered something about God's promises and about God's keeping power and about God's delivering power. Peter discovered something about doing the impossible. Peter discovered that obedience brings adventure and even exhilaration. Peter discovered that he could call on Jesus when it looked like he was about to go under. While Peter did get wet, I believe it is always better to be a wet Peter than a dry Thomas.

When Peter and Jesus got back in the boat, the storm ceased, and they all worshiped Him. In life, we learn the lesson then take the test. God does the opposite: We take the test then learn the lesson. So what lessons can all of Jesus' disciples learn about their experience on the boat that day? First, we can learn that seeming adversities can be opportunities for adventure. Second, through Christ we can stand buoyant on trials that at one time would have caused us to sink, like criticism, fear, persecution, and jealousy. Third, we can learn that Jesus' disciples may not know where He is at all times, but thankfully, He always knows where we are. He is the Good Shepherd who cares for and watches over His sheep. Fourth, when we grow in Christ, the things that used to sink us, can't take us under. Fifth, disciples might get down, but in Jesus we will not go under. Sixth, it is better to risk something for God and falter than to do nothing and succeed. Seventh, the turtle only moves ahead when he has his neck out. In other words, sometimes we have to stick our neck out for God. Finally, in the Chinese alphabet, the symbol for danger, is also the symbol of opportunity. We must be willing to take great risks if we desire to have great adventures with the Lord.

Isn't this the carpenter? Isn't this Mary's son and the brother of James, Joseph, Judas and Simon? Aren't his sisters here with us?" And they took offense at him.

REJECTION

Mark 6:3

Although Jesus had done many miraculous deeds throughout the region, and strongly desired to exercise His power to help and heal among His own, He experienced rejection simply by doing the work of His Father.

After the NBA championship game in 2000, the Los Angeles Lakers returned to L.A. and received a hero's welcome. Some 550,000 Lakers fans poured out into the streets of Los Angeles to welcome home the definitive champions. These adoring fans were euphoric with jubilation and celebration, and understandably so, because they were the champions. They were the repeat champions that had won in such an impressive way, defeating Sacramento four games, and then sweeping San Antonio four games, and on to defeat the Philadelphia 76ers. No team had accumulated as many victories en route to the championship as these L.A. Lakers. And so understandably, the town came out to welcome home their defending champions.

Can you imagine how different it might have been if LA had remained quiet after the Lakers returned? Imagine how bizarre it would have been if there had been no one on the streets to greet the Lakers when they returned—no banners, no parades, no fanfare, no graffiti. Can you imagine how it might have been if immediately after the Lakers' win, life in Los Angeles had resumed as normal, as though nothing had happened? How do you think Shaquille O'Neal would feel if he had been walking down the street after winning a NBA championship and no one said congratulations? How would Kobe Bryant have felt if he were to walk into a restaurant and no one said, "Hey, there's Kobe Bryant, a champion!"?

Think about how strange it would have felt if in every city the Lakers visited after their win everyone celebrated what they had done, including the teams they had defeated, and all had parades for the Lakers, but when they returned home to Los Angeles, no one greeted them. That would be bizarre, would it not?

Just such a bizarre event happened to Jesus, according to Mark 6:3. The last sentence reads "and so they rejected him." The they in this verse is Jesus' hometown folks in Nazareth. For one whole year Jesus had been doing ministry in the region. For one year he had been teaching in the synagogues to great crowds of people. Billy Graham-crusade-sized crowds had come to hear Nazareth's hometown boy as he illuminated the truths of our God. For one year they had experienced His mighty deeds of healing; the lame experienced restoration of their limbs, those who were blind received their sight, the deaf were hearing, and lepers were cleansed and readmitted into society.

It was a world-shaking ministry that Jesus had established and His fame had spread throughout Galilee (Mark 1:28). The Scriptures reveal that Jesus returned to His home village of Nazareth and was not well received. It is sad that He was rejected by those people, especially since they were the people He had grown up with. Nazareth was not even a city, just a hamlet. Cartographers (mapmakers)

The Scriptures reveal that Jesus returned to His home village of Nazareth and was not well received.

would have a difficult time putting a star by Nazareth. It was one of those little villages that if you blinked, you would miss.

No one of stature came from Nazareth. No prominent rabbi, no great teacher, no one who had his name on the social register claimed to have emanated from Nazareth. In fact, when Nathaniel, one of Jesus' first disciples, heard that the Messiah was Jesus of Nazareth, he asked, "Can any good thing come from Nazareth?" (John 1:46).

When I think of Nazareth, I think of the movie "Hoosier," starring Gene Hackman. The movie is about a high school basketball team in the little town if Hickory, Indiana. The town was so small that the townspeople put the "o-r-y" on the end of Hickory to give the town some dignity. It was Hick-ory and there everybody was a hillbilly. The basketball team played in a converted barn that had been turned into a sports arena. They were people somewhat like Larry Byrd, who was born in the Indiana town of French Lick. They were backward, tobacco-chewing hillbillies from Hickory, but they could play some basketball.

Hickory won their regional championship and advanced to the Sweet 16 of the Indiana state basketball tournament. When they got off the bus from Hickory, if the vehicle could accurately be called a bus, they realized that all the other teams, brothas included, from towns like Muncie and Gary were impressive. The Hickory players, with their primitive dress and uncouth ways, seemed a far cry from the more impressive teams from larger towns. When they went into the arena, because they were accustomed to playing in a barn, they looked up at the ceiling of the Indianapolis Coliseum and said, "My God. We didn't think they had anything this big." Gene Hackman, their coach, sensed that they were intimidated by the size of the coliseum. He measured the length between the floor and the goal and said, "You know what? The goal here is 10 feet from the ground, just like in the barn in Hickory." Then he measured the inside of the basket cylinder and informed them that it too was the same size as the cylinder in Hickory. The same size equipment was just housed in a bigger barn.

When Hickory got onto the court with their Larry Byrds, they drove the Muncie team crazy. They drove Indianapolis crazy. The team from Gary was crazy. With all the big city teams as their opponents, the hillbilly team from Hickory won the state finals.

What are the implications of not being received by our own?

When I think of Hickory, I think of Jesus' hometown of Nazareth, the Hickory of Galilee. When Jesus returned home, having done so well, one might expect that He would have received the same type of reception from the home crowd that the Lakers received when they returned to Los Angeles. One might expect that Jesus' homecoming after one year of successful ministry would have included parades, people lining the streets, banners, flags, trumpets blowing, and proclamations being read. One might expect that the city council would have given Him the key to the city of Nazareth. One might have expected that the mayor would have proclaimed Jesus Day in Nazareth.

John's Gospel says in his prologue that Jesus came to His own and His own did not receive Him. What are the implications of not being received by our own? When Jesus returned to Nazareth, he taught in the synagogue. When they heard Him teach with such profundity, insight, and illumination, they began to wonder, "Where did He get all this wisdom?" And the emphasis is on the word He. If it had been a man from some other village, they would never have asked the question. Familiarity breeds contempt, as the old saying goes. Because Jesus had emerged from among them, they questioned His abilities. They were not asking, "Where did He get all this wisdom?" They were really wondering, "Where did He get all this wisdom and knowledge?" They knew He didn't get it from the library at Nazareth, because there was none. They knew he didn't get it at the high school in Nazareth, because there was no high school. And they knew he didn't get it at the University in Nazareth, because U of N didn't exist. Nazareth was just another small town like Hickory.

The question that the Nazarenes asked about Jesus is the same question that is asked of us at some time or another: "Where did she get...?" The townspeople were trying to cast a shadow of suspicion on Jesus. Some even said that the reason Jesus was so wise was because He was in league with the devil. There were some citizens of Nazareth who just couldn't believe that this boy from among them could teach like Jesus did. Since they could not dissect Him and figure out where He got His wisdom, they moved from dissecting Him to diminishing Him. They asked four questions. The first question was "Hey, wait a minute! Where did He get all this wisdom?" And in verse 3, they asked the question, "Isn't He the carpenter?" Then they questioned His paternity: "Isn't that Mary's son?" Finally, they questioned his family's status: "Don't his sisters and brothers still live right here?"

Nazareth's response to Jesus tells us something about the Messiah, His profession, His occupation, and His location. We must never lose sight of the fact that the One whom we worship is a blue-collar worker. He did

There were some citizens of Nazareth who just couldn't believe that this boy from among them could teach like Jesus did.

not have His name in the Galilean social register. For years He had been the local carpenter for the people of His hick town. He had spent much of His 30 years there in the carpentry business. Any time a chair had needed fixing, they would take it to Jesus' carpentry shop. When they had a table leg that was broken, they would take it to Jesus. When a farmer had a wagon that broke down or a yoke that had broken, he would take it to Jesus' carpentry shop, and He would fix it. The great Scottish New Testament scholar William Barclay has argued that Jesus probably had this on the outside of His shop: "If you've got a yoke to get fixed, bring it to Me, because My yoke is easy."

So after all of those years of serving the carpentry needs of the good people of Nazareth, Jesus returned after His yearlong absence. Upon His return, Jesus was standing in their synagogue, teaching with such profundity, insight, and illumination that they could not help but wonder how such a transformation had occurred in such a short time.

When the heir apparent to the throne of England begins his grooming to become king, he is sent to Scotland. There he is trained as the Prince of Wales. While in Scotland the prince is taught many manners, including etiquette, diplomacy, and foreign languages. When Joseph Kennedy, the patriarch of America's "royal family," determined that his boys would be world-class leaders he sent all of them to prep schools—Joseph, who was killed in World War II; John, who became president; and Robert and Teddy, both senators. All of them eventually went to prestigious Ivy League schools like Harvard. That is the way potential leaders are trained. They are sent to preparatory school before they enter Harvard, Oxford, Yale, or some other prestigious institution of higher learning. But look at how God treated His own Son, the King of kings. He didn't send Him to Scotland. God didn't send Jesus to an exclusive prep school. Instead, Jesus was born in a Bethlehem stable, not in a prestigious hotel or hospital. Following His birth, Jesus was taken off to Egypt just so that His life could be spared.

When His earthly parents headed back to the region to live, they ended up in Hickory.

When God's Son and His earthly parents settled in Nazareth, things didn't get any better. Instead of enrolling in an elite university, Jesus became Joseph's apprentice at the carpentry shop. Jesus had no degrees on his wall. He was not a Pi Kappa Alpha or any great Greek frat man. He was neither lettered nor scholarly. He had been fixing tables and chairs. He was the prophet of Nazareth. And not knowing His true heritage or inheritance, the townsfolk tried to remind Jesus of who he was. And they tried to diminish Him by asking, "Isn't He the carpenter?" They wanted to know, "How did you get so wise? After all, you're nothing but a carpenter."

Ironically, they were telling the truth. They didn't mean it to compliment Jesus; they meant it to diminish him. Indeed, He had been in the carpentry business for as long as they had known Him. Jesus is the Carpenter of our lives. Although one day He hung up His hammer and saw, took off his apron, and stored away His nails, Jesus never got out of the carpentry business. The truth of the matter is that Jesus is still fixing things. He's a fixing man. He no longer fixes tables and chairs, but He'll fix you and me. He's the carpenter of the broken hearted. He knows how to repair messed-up folks.

To taunt Him further they asked another question. They went from trying to diminish Jesus to trying to smear him. Their second question was, "Isn't that Mary's son?" They weren't looking for information. They were trying to smear Him because in those days when a boy

Jesus never got out of the carpentry business. The truth of the matter is that Jesus is still fixing things.

was introduced he was identified with his father. So if the people of Nazareth had been sincere, they should have called Jesus the son of Joseph. Remember Simon Bar-jona? The word bar means "son" in Hebrew and Aramaic. Simon was the son of John. Remember James and John, the sons of Zebedee? But this crowd asked, "Isn't this Mary's son?" Because they were hometown folks, they remembered that some 30 years earlier when Jesus was born, His mother Mary became pregnant while still engaged. They remembered that she had gone to visit her cousin Elizabeth, and during the three months she was away her pregnancy became more apparent.

Mary tried to tell everybody that what happened: "I saw the angel Gabriel. He told me that I was carrying the Christ child. And I asked him how could this thing be because I didn't know any man yet. Gabriel told me that the Holy Spirit would overshadow me and the Most High would come upon me. I tried to tell them, but nobody would believe me." About 30 years later, the good people of Nazareth were trying to throw up Jesus' unorthodox conception in His face. They were telling Him, "Not only are you nothing but a carpenter, you are an illegitimate, bastard son. You don't even know who your daddy is."

Their other rationale for devaluing Jesus centered on the fact that His brothers, James, Joseph, Judas and Simon, and sisters had never left Nazareth. In other words, Jesus couldn't be all that because if He was really all that, why didn't His brothers and sisters ever amount to anything? Jesus' family was no better than their families. "All of His family members are ignorant just like us," they must have thought. "His family members are dumb like us. They still live in Hickory. None of them are on the social register. They live over on Maple Street. Their homes don't even have central air. They use the city bus line just like us."

In essence, what they were saying was their hometown boy was nothing but a carpenter, a bastard son whose family didn't amount to anything. That's the problem with the folks who live in Hickory. The minute we rise above Hickory, there's always going to be somebody who is going to throw the past up in our face—who we used to be, what we used to do. We don't have to put a lid on the crabs in a bucket in order to keep them in because when one crab tries to climb out of the bucket, those still stuck inside the bucket will reach up and pull it back down. That is a Hickory mindset.

Many people have experienced this same phenomenon. As long as an alcoholic stays drunk as a skunk, nobody says a word. As long as a person is falling, nobody says a thing. As long as a person doesn't have a job, nobody complains about anything. But the minute that person hears the Gospel and begins to turn around, the same folks who once had no opinion will say, "Hey, you ain't nothing but a carpenter. You don't know who your daddy is." "You ain't nothing but a drunk! You used to hang out on the corner." "You ain't nothing but whore. I know about the men you've slept with."

Jesus has all power. He had it then and He has it now. Yet, when He went to Nazareth something happened to His power. His power was short-circuited there. When He went to heal, He couldn't heal. For some reason, when He went to preach, nobody got blessed. He couldn't do any miracles in Nazareth because of their unbelief. That lets me know that what God is able to do in our lives is predicated on what we allow Him to do.

The minute we rise above Hickory, there's always going to be somebody who is going to throw the past up in our face...

Human beings have two choices. We can either release God's power, or we can restrict God's power. And what determines whether or not God's power has been released or restricted is faith. The lack of faith—the lack of anticipation—of not having the right attitude, restricts God's power. The sun can melt wax, and the sun can harden mud. The same sun, but two different reactions. Just like the sun can melt one thing and harden another, in the presence of divinity some folk's hearts get melted, some hearts get chapped, and some hearts get hard.

Some people leave church and say, "I didn't get anything out of it." Although the person professes to have gotten nothing, the problem is not the preacher, the choir, or the usher board. Every worshiper must bring something to the plate in order to receive something. Some people show up at church thinking they are doing God a favor just to be seen. They don't come seeking deliverance or blessings; they just show up. They come to be amused or entertained.

Sometimes the people we think will accept us are the same folks who reject us.

These are the same kinds of folk that the Bible says restricted Jesus' power by rejecting Him. Jesus was rejected by His own hometown. He knows what rejection feels like. He understands our pain when we experience rejection. And in this passage He teaches us how to handle rejection. Sometimes the people we think will accept us are the same folks who reject us.

But Jesus was probably thinking, "I know if anybody's going to receive Me, the folks in Nazareth will. I mean, after all, I'm one of them. I grew up in their midst." If anybody could know Jesus, who could have known Him better than the people of Nazareth? He had been there for 30 years. He had fixed their tables and their chairs. They knew what kind of a man he was. They knew something about his character. They knew He never told a lie. They knew he never ripped off anybody. They knew that when Jesus fixed a table, He fixed it right. He didn't cheat anybody. They knew that when He was a teenager, He never messed over a young girl. They knew how polite He was. They knew that He helped senior citizens across the street. If anybody should have accepted Jesus, it was the people of Nazareth.

The Scriptures do not say that someone the butchers or the barbers rejected has become the chief stone, because butchers and barbers don't know everything about stones. Jesus said the Stone that the builders—the experts who know about construction—rejected has become the Cornerstone. This means that the experts are not always right. Just because somebody says, "You are a reject" doesn't mean that person is right. And just because somebody says "You're not going to amount to anything" doesn't mean the pronouncement is right.

Jesus said the Stone that the builders, the experts who know about construction, rejected has become the Cornerstone.

An interviewer once asked famed music composer/producer Quincy Jones if he had ever misjudged a new talent. Jones replied, "Yes, I told Luther Vandross that he didn't have what it took to make it as a solo act." Yet, today Luther draws thousands as a solo artist. His CD sales have gone platinum and beyond. No, the experts are not always right. Consider that after Fred Astaire's first screen test, a 1933 memo from the MGM testing director said: "Can't act. Slightly bald. Can dance a little." Astaire kept that memo over the fireplace in his

Beverly Hills home. Another expert proven wrong. An expert said of famous football coach Vince Lombardi: "He possesses minimal football knowledge. Lacks motivation." Louisa May Alcott, the author of *Little Women*, was advised by her family to find work as a servant or seamstress.

The experts may reject us, but that does not mean we should stop at their opinion. Beethoven handled the violin awkwardly and preferred playing his own compositions instead of improving his technique. His teacher called him utterly hopeless as a composer. The teacher of the celebrated opera singer Enrico Caruso said that Caruso had no voice at all and could not sing. Walt Disney was fired from a newspaper for lacking ideas. He also went bankrupt several times before he built Disneyland. Eighteen publishers turned down Richard Bach's 10,000-word story about a soaring seagull before Macmillan finally published it in 1970. By 1975, *Jonathan Livingston Seagull* had sold more than seven million copies in the U.S. alone. The music industry once referred to a now famous female singing group as "the no-hit Supremes." The experts were wrong about them. The experts were even wrong about Sammy Sosa, the home run king. Sosa used to play baseball for the Texas Rangers, but President George W. Bush, who then owned the Rangers, told Sammy Sosa, "You can't bat." And Bush traded him to the Chicago Cubs. Sosa has been knocking home runs ever since. Experts have an important function in our lives, but they are not always right.

We have a choice. We do not have to internalize rejection, even at the hands of experts. But even so, rejection is not the end of the world. It wasn't the end of the world for Jesus when the citizens of Nazareth rejected him, and it doesn't have to be the end for us. Although Jesus was perplexed by their rejection of Him, He was not paralyzed. He didn't understand it, but it did not disable Him. Many times when folks reject us we get paralyzed. It is one thing to be perplexed, but it is quite another thing to be paralyzed.

I know some people who do not like me. I don't know why they do not like me. But I also understand that I don't have to do anything to somebody in order for that person to dislike me. Rejection is heartbreaking. But Jesus helped me to understand that heartbreak doesn't have to paralyze me. Nowhere in the text does it record that Jesus begged the Nazarenes to love Him after they rejected Him. Nowhere did He say, "Please accept me." Nowhere in the text does it state that He was crying, "I want you to receive me." Jesus' own brothers and sisters didn't believe Him, but He didn't even beg them to accept Him. The Bible says that when He got rejected in Nazareth, He moved on to the next town. And that is what His followers ought to do. When we get rejected, we should go to the next town. If they don't receive us in Nazareth, we can move on to another place.

Jesus' actions indicate, as the old saying goes, "One monkey don't stop no show." There's more than one fish in the pond. When one door of opportunity closes, God has a window open somewhere else. When we lose one friend, God has another friend. In fact, God's got so many blessings that He can give us—over here and over there. God blessed the ministry of His Son. Jesus went on to perform many miracles and comfort many broken hearts. Now, He sits at the right hand of the Father.

There is a familiar story of unknown origin about a man who was a collector of great works of art. He had works from all the great masters—Rembrandt, Picasso,

Nowhere in the text does it record that Jesus begged the Nazarenes to love Him after they rejected Him.

Van Goegh, da Vinci, Michelangelo, Monet, Renoir, Raphael, and many others. The man truly loved his art collection. But one thing the man treasured more than his valuable art collection was his only son. But the man lost his son during the war in Vietnam. One day, a young man rang the man's doorbell. It was a soldier who had served in the war with the man's son. The young soldier and the son had become like brothers in Vietnam. In fact, the son had saved the soldier's life during the war. The soldier had drawn a portrait of the son, and he wanted the father to have it. The portrait was good, but nothing like the work of the masters. Still, the man treasured the portrait of his son more than he did any of the great works of art he owned.

The father cried and hung that portrait in a prominent place in his house. A few years later, the father himself died, and willed that all his art would all be sold at auction, including the portrait of his son. On the day of the auction, the hall was filled with collectors from around the world wanting a chance to bid on the works of the masters. The auctioneer began by explaining that the man's will stipulated that the portrait of his son be auctioned first. The great art collectors rejected the portrait immediately. They had come for the works of the masters, not the work of an amateur. They wouldn't even consider making a bid.

A voice in the back of the room shouted. "We want to see the famous paintings. Skip this one." But the auctioneer persisted. "Will someone bid for this painting? Who will start the bidding? $100, $200?" Another voice shouted angrily, "We didn't come to see this painting. We came to see the Van Goghs, the Rembrandts. Get on with the real bids!" But still the auctioneer continued. "The son! The son! Who'll take the son?"

Finally, a voice came from the very back of the room. It was the long-time gardener of the man and his son. "I'll give $10 for the painting."

Being a man of modest means, it was all he could afford. "We have $10, who will bid $20?" Someone shouted, "Give it to him for $10. Let us see the masters." The auctioneer said, "$10 is the bid, won't someone bid $20?" The crowd grew angry. They didn't want the picture of the son. They wanted more worthy investments for their collections. Finally, the auctioneer pounded the gavel. "Going once, twice, SOLD for $10!" A man sitting on the second row shouted. "Now let's get on with the collection!"

The auctioneer laid down his gavel. "I'm sorry, the auction is over." Gasps were heard throughout the room. "What about the paintings?" someone asked. "I am sorry," the auctioneer explained. "When I was called to conduct this auction, I was told of a stipulation in the will that I was not allowed to reveal until this time. Only the painting of the son was to be auctioned. Whoever bought that painting would inherit the man's entire estate, including the paintings. So you see, the man who took the son gets everything!"

God gave His son 2,000 years ago to die on a cruel cross. Much like the auctioneer, His message today is: "The son, the son, who'll take the son?" Because whoever takes the Son gets everything.

But a Samaritan, as he traveled, came where the man was; and when he saw him, he took pity on him.

Luke 10:33, NIV

MERCY

Luke 9:51-55; 10:25-37

The Samaritan man, in doing what is right, was an agent of God's mercy, allowing the fallen man to experience divine mercy through a human act of mercy.

Of all the stories Jesus told none has captured the human imagination like the parable of the Good Samaritan. Its message and meaning have penetrated various groups within society. To test the scope of the parable's popularity, a survey was done to determine how many people actually knew the story of the Good Samaritan. Surprisingly, over 50 percent of those queried knew something about the story. That is pretty amazing considering the fact that we live in an age of biblical illiteracy. It very well may be the best known parable in the world.

The phrase Good Samaritan is a colloquialism, a part of our common speech that can be found in many dictionaries. There are hospitals named "Good Samaritan," identifying themselves as caregivers to the injured and downtrodden. There are certain laws and statutes on the books called Good Samaritan laws, requiring people to render aid and assistance during a time of distress. In the final episode of the television show "Seinfeld," Jerry goes to jail for not helping someone in a carjacking. He refused to be a Good Samaritan. That the term "Good Samaritan" is well known may be its great problem. It may, in fact, be too well known. We've heard it so much that we are unable to hear its power. It's like a painting that has hung on the wall for many years. We've looked at it so much that we don't look at it any more. We fail to notice it until someone comes along and remarks on the painting, reminding us of its beauty and power.

We should read the parable of the Good Samaritan frequently to help us appreciate the beauty of what Jesus was teaching us. The story is a snapshot of what we find whenever people come together. This is a masterful story because in it we find three fundamental philosophies of life whenever people come together. They are found in every culture, in every community, in every age. So, in the story of the Good Samaritan, Jesus told of an old road that went down from Jerusalem to Jericho. He put a few people on it who were taking a walk, and gave us a snapshot of the world community.

On the road to Jericho, we will find three kinds of people: those who abuse people, those who avoid people, and those who assist people.

The Abusers

A woman complained to her exterminator that the bugs in her house would not stay away. He told her, "Ma'am, the reason is quite simple. You see, wherever people go, bugs go." The same is true for Abusers. Wherever there are people, there are others seeking to abuse them. Abusers are pests and predators who must go where people go, otherwise there would be no one for them to abuse. Throughout human history there have been Abusers, both famous and infamous, known and unknown. History records men like Caligula, Adolph Hitler, and Slobidan Milosovitch. Some Abusers are less menacing, choosing to wreak havoc on their victims financially, not socially, politically, or physically. Most of the world's Abusers are not known by name, although their prototype is quite common. The man who beats his wife is an abuser. The woman who locks her children in the car while she enters a motel room to party is an abuser. Another kind of abuser is the drug-addicted grandson who threatens his grand-mother in order to get money from her. An abuser is a so-called friend who borrows but never gives.

A certain man went down the road to Jericho, a city located 1000 feet below sea level and 17 miles from Jerusalem, which is 22,000 feet above sea level. The difference in elevation between the two cities made it a downward road. When I went to Israel several years ago, we visited Jerusalem during January. The temperature was about 35 degrees. From there we went down to Jericho where there were palm trees swaying in 80 degree weather. So the distance between Jerusalem and Jericho is a precipitous drop. Not only that, it is a dangerous drop. During Jesus' time, it was called the "bloody way" because it was a haven for thieves, bandits, and desperados. They would hide in caves, ravines, and caverns in order to prey upon unsuspecting travelers as they made their way from Jerusalem to Jericho. The road to Jericho was like traveling in the worst part of a city—a crime-infested, lawless region. In Jesus' parable, the Abusers pounced on an unsuspecting victim who was probably a Hebrew.

The man in the story was a victim of the road. The thieves did three things to abuse him. First they beat him, which means he was badly bloodied and bruised. They had to beat him up enough that he wouldn't put up any resistance. He may have had a broken jaw and possibly broken ribs. After they beat him, they robbed him of his possessions, which probably included his clothing. After brutalizing the Samaritan and taking all that he had, they left him to die. The Bible says he "fell into the hands" of these Abusers. The word translated "fell" here is the same verb used to describe an ambush. It is the same verb (*peirasmos*) used in chapter two, verse two of the Book of James (from which we also get the word pirate). It means something that came without warning.

Abusers often come without warning, like the Abusers that snuffed out the life of Ennis Cosby. Bill Cosby's young son was simply changing his flat tire when he fell into the hands of Abusers who killed him because they wanted what he had. Michael Jordan's father, James, fell into the hands of Abusers who at any price were determined to deprive the basketball superstar's father of his possessions. These kinds of pirates share the same philosophy as other Abusers who have inflicted pain on humanity. It is the philosophy of men like Adolph Hitler, of gang members who prey on weak, impoverished communities, and of underworld crime networks like the Mafia. But this philosophy is also that of the unscrupulous car salesperson, the fraudulent insurance representative, and the predatory accountant who embezzles the hard-earned money of a trusting client. Predators are the dishonest repairmen who cheat their customers, and they are the beautiful con artists who bilk lonely old men of their retirement reserves. The abuser is a predator who lives by this philosophy: "What's yours is mine and I'm going to take it." What the abuser takes may be money, self-respect, or one's reputation in the community.

The abuser is a predator who lives by this philosophy: "What's yours is mine and I'm going to take it."

Abusers are everywhere. There are different kinds of abuse and Abusers to fit every type. Some Abusers are not perceived as readily as others. Any of us can become Abusers simply by our actions. When we cheat on our income taxes, or when we lie about our children's ages to get the 12-and-under discount at the buffet, we become Abusers of trust. Likewise, the employee who takes pens, paper clips, and paper, or the worker who falsifies time sheets or expense reports, or the employee who doesn't put in a full day's work for a full day's pay is guilty of abusing the trust given by the employer. Shoppers who return clothes after they have bought and worn them are guilty of being Abusers. Murderers abuse the sacredness of life that they have no power to create.

People who live according to the "what's-yours-is-mine" philosophy live according to an entitlement philosophy. They feel no guilt for taking. They don't say, "thank you." They think it is their right and privilege to take from unsuspecting victims. They look at their victims and think, "If you're too stupid to figure out what's going on, then that's too bad. I don't have any responsibility to be honest with you."

Matthew Henry, the famous commentary author, was robbed once. After the robbery, instead of feeling bitterness or regret, he was thankful. Henry indicated three reasons why he felt gratitude after the robbery. First, he said he was grateful that the robber took his money, but not his life. Second, he was grateful that although the thief took his money, he still had some financial resources left. And finally, Henry said he was grateful that the robbers were the ones who stole from him; he had not stolen from them.

The Avoiders

The Avoiders share a different philosophy from the Abusers; nevertheless, theirs is no better. The Avoider's philosophy is: "What is mine, is mine, and I'm going to keep it." Theirs is a philosophy of indifference. Abusers deliberately commit their sinful deeds at the expense of others. Avoiders, however, are generally guilty of the sin of omission. Theirs is the sin of Dives, who refused to acknowledge the humanity of poor Lazarus, let alone come to his aid (Luke 16:19-31). The rich man went to hell for doing nothing. First John 3:17 says: "If anyone has material possessions and sees his brother in need but has no pity on him, how can the love of God be in him?"

There were two Avoiders in the story of the Good Samaritan. One was a priest who also was traveling down the road to Jericho. He was coming back from Jerusalem where the Temple stood. So even though the priest had been in church, probably singing something like, "This little light of mine, I'm gonna let it shine," when the benediction was pronounced his faith was challenged. The authenticity and integrity of his religion were challenged by this man on the roadside. Any religion that allows shouting on Sunday, and lets us disregard those in need on Monday is a bogus religion. It's not how high we can jump and shout that matters; it is how we walk after we come down from shouting. He had just left church, but when the priest saw the injured man, he moved to the other side of the road. So his worship experience at the Temple apparently had made no impact on him.

After the priest came a Levite. Now, Levitical law declared that anyone who touched a dead body would be rendered ceremonially unclean (Numbers 19:11-16). That's why Jesus' touching the dead son of the widow in Luke 7 was so significant. Jesus always put people over policies. But this Levite was not about to risk his status to help an injured stranger. That's the problem with a lot of Christians today. Many of us are of little use to the Kingdom because we are unwilling to risk our standing in the church or community to help someone in need. But the Levite did more than the priest did in that he actually went over and looked at the injured man. A lot of folks are like that Levite—they come over to meddle in your business. They're not going to help you do anything. They just want to look at you and be nosy. They go to funerals, not because they knew the deceased, nor because they care about the bereaved. They show up because they want to meddle. Avoiders are not going to help, but they want to know who else was there. They want to know how much money was spent on the funeral. They want to know how many flowers were sent and from whom. Avoiders will meddle in another person's life, and then pass on without ever trying to ease that person's suffering. They don't want to get involved. They want to remain neutral. But God will judge us all as much for what we don't do as He will for what we do.

Avoiders are not found just among unbelievers. There are many ways that Christians are Avoiders. Our communities are filled with problems, but Christians avoid them. Our schools are failing to educate our children, but we don't want to get involved. There are crack houses strewn throughout inner city America, but we do nothing. Dr. Martin Luther King Jr. said that all good people have to do for evil to reign is nothing. Evil thrives on nonchalance. Apathy is an evildoer's incubator. That's what happened in pre-World War II. Evil was running rampant in Germany under the reign of Hitler, but the church folks there did nothing. The Lutherans were there, but they did nothing. Someone asked the Lutheran pastor Martin Niemoeller why the Lutherans didn't do something to stop Hitler. How did one man orchestrate and implement a total reign of terror and destruction? Niemoeller explained, "It was easy. Hitler first came for the communists in 1933, and I was not a communist so I didn't say anything. Then Hitler came for the trade unionists, but since I was not a trade unionist, I didn't say anything. Then he came for the gypsies, but since there were no gypsies in my family I really didn't care what happened to them. Then he came for the mentally and physically handicapped, but since it didn't affect anyone that I knew, I didn't say anything. Then he came for the Jews. I wasn't a Jew, so I didn't say anything. But then Hitler came for me, and there was no one left to speak up on my behalf!"

Avoiders are not found just among unbelievers. There are many ways that Christians are Avoiders.

The inaction of the Avoiders in the Good Samaritan parable is even more shameful when we consider the fact that in Jesus' day, priests were also trained as physicians. So this priest was board certified and trained in emergency medical techniques, yet both he and the Levite chose to ignore their training and their faith, and kept walking down the road. They were so interested in getting down the road that they missed what was on the road. We can do that, too. We can be so consumed with going on our own way that we neglect that which we encounter along the way. First Timothy 6:18 tells us, "Command them to do good, to be rich in good deeds, and to be generous and willing to share."

Why was the German public condemned for allowing Hitler's murderous reign to run rampant? Even those who did not kill were condemned for doing nothing. The shame of the church has not been criminal activity. The shame of the church is its unwillingness to adequately address the evils infecting our society: abortion, pornography, discrimination, and all kinds of abuse.

The Assisters

Jesus says in verse 33 that a Samaritan came and had compassion on the man. The Samaritan cared for his wounds, chauffeured him to the nearest inn, paid for his accommodations, and left with a promise to take care of the remaining balance upon his return. Jesus said, "a certain Samaritan," although we call him the "Good Samaritan." Using the word good in conjunction with the word Samaritan was an oxymoron for a Jew. No Jew in Jesus' day would have ever used the adjective good to describe a Samaritan. Jews and Samaritans were bitter enemies. Samaritans were at the bottom both socially and religiously. The Jews despised the Samaritans because they were half-breeds. The Samaritans had peculiar ways and customs. They had their own temple. In His day, calling someone a Samaritan was an expression of derision. James and John wanted to incinerate them. Their name was a racial epithet. After Jesus made the claim that he had come from God, in John 8:48, the Jews chided him, "Aren't we right in saying that you are a Samaritan and demon-possessed?" The woman at the well was a Samaritan. The Bible tells us that Jews and Samaritans had no dealings with each other.

This is where Jesus threw a curve ball in the parable. He described with some detail how the Samaritan mercifully cared for the injured man's wounds—rubbing oil on his wounds. And verse 35 gives another bit of subtle detail about the Samaritan's compassion. It tells us that the next day he gave the innkeeper two silver coins, two days' wages, to pay him for keeping the injured man. The Samaritan didn't just take the injured man to the inn and drop him off. In order to give the innkeeper the coins the next day, he must have stayed with the man overnight.

So the Assisters have a totally different philosophy than the Abusers and the Avoiders. Their philosophy is "What is mine is yours, and I'm going to share it with you." So, again, what happened? The Abusers beat the man up. The Avoiders passed the man up. But the Assister picked him up and thereby became an agent of divine mercy. Wherever we go in life, we will encounter people who will beat us up, and others who will pass us up. But God always has people who will pick us up.

We are accustomed to considering this story from the perspective of the Samaritan, the priest, or the Levite.

Wherever we go in life, we will encounter people who will beat us up, and others who will pass us up. But God always has people who will pick us up.

One day, I decided to ask the Holy Spirit to allow me to interview the injured man. He was a Jew, entrenched in his culture and religion. He grew up inhaling the fumes of racism and hatred for the Samaritans. The Holy Spirit allowed me to ask him, "Man, what happened?" The man told me, "I was badly beaten up and left in a semi-conscious state. My teeth were knocked out all along the road. I was lying there praying to God like I had never prayed before. I said, 'Lord, please send somebody by here.' Well, I just knew God had answered my prayer when I saw the minister coming down the road. I was just so sure that the church folks were going to help me. But you know what happened? The church folks just passed right on by me. Then here came the deacon. I thought to myself, 'Oh, help has arrived. The deacon goes to church every Sunday. He'll stop and help me.' My spirits lifted when he paused, and then dashed just as quickly when he kept on walking. But then I looked up and I heard the baying of a donkey. I heard the footsteps clicking along the cobblestones of the Jericho road. I looked up and said, 'Oh, my God. There's a Samaritan. I know the Samaritans are cruel people. He's probably going to beat up on me some more. My parents taught me all about them. They steal, and they're evil. They're no good. They can't be trusted.' Then I braced myself because I just knew that he was carrying a knife. When he reached in his traveling pouch, I thought he was reaching for a weapon. But instead of a knife, he pulled out oil and wine. I never thought a Samaritan would be the one God would choose to rescue me. At that moment, everything my culture had taught me was blown away. I didn't understand it."

What I learned from my spiritual retrospective with the injured man was that we believers need to be careful. We never know what channel God is going to use as our blessing. Very often God will send to us the very kind of person we despise. But why? He sends the despised for the sake of our own growth. He sends the despised at our weakest moment because only then are we willing to submit so that our mind and heart can be opened to extend mercy. God will send the despised to us just to remind us that He is no respecter of persons.

When I was in the seventh grade, my sister and I were the only black students at Mamie S. Wagner Junior High School in suburban Louisville, Kentucky. Except for the custodian, we were the only two blacks at the school. But faithfully we went every day, even though we were afraid. And to be sure, there were some Abusers at the school. They laughed at us. They laughed at our culture. Their ridicule was hurtful, but what also hurt was the inaction of the Avoiders. They knew what was going on, but they turned away and did nothing. I survived that experience because there were some white people there who were Assisters. They respected my humanity and my culture. The Assisters wanted to know more about me and my culture, and they shared theirs with me.

That experience taught me that our greatest witness for Christ is not our talk, but our walk of mercy. The world's greatest sermon will not come from the pulpit, but from the testimony given when the preaching is over. We are called by Jesus to take the walk of mercy. The Good Samaritan took the walk of mercy. That was his ministry.

Timothy J. Keller, author of *Ministries of Mercy* (P&R Publishing Company, 1997), has offered a succinct definition of mercy: "meeting a felt need with deeds." According to him, people have four basic needs: physical, social, psychological, and spiritual. But according to

The world's greatest sermon will not come from the pulpit, but from the testimony given when the preaching is over.

Augustine, the core need that all people have is spiritual. A felt need is one that we are aware of. A lot of people are not aware that they have spiritual needs. They know that something is wrong, but they don't know what's bothering them.

The goal of evangelical Christianity is to reach the core need—the spiritual need. But the walk of mercy begins with the felt need. Until we minister to the felt need, we can never reach the core need. While persons may not be aware of their need for God, for forgiveness, or for reconciliation with God, they are aware that they have need for food, clothing, and shelter.

That we have more basic spiritual needs is evidenced in the fact that many of us are lonely.

That we have more basic spiritual needs is evidenced in the fact that many of us are lonely. We are suspicious and afraid to have a trusting relationship with anybody. We have anxieties, with no real sense of purpose. The world has told us that the answer to those deeper needs is found in gratifying the physical. Satisfying a spiritual need with a physical bandage has only a temporary effect. Engaging in illicit sex to ease loneliness is a temporary solution. Engaging in reckless behavior to deny our suspicious and untrusting nature is folly. It's like giving a Lexus®, a house, money, and jewelry to a fish. With all of these things, the fish is still unfulfilled if he's out of water. A fish belongs in water. He needs water to survive, and nothing will substitute. And so it is with God. People need God to survive, and nothing else will do. Too many of us have bought into the lie of materialism.

Ministries of mercy is not about meeting felt need with pious talk. In 1 John 3:18 it reads: "Dear children, let us not love with words or tongue but with actions and in truth." The Samaritan felt the man's pain—he was hurt, dehydrated, and sore. He ministered to every need the injured man had, including his spiritual need. The victimized man needed to open his heart to God's ways, and not have a mind closed by human laws. The doorway to reaching a person's spiritual needs is first meeting their felt needs. It is the best avenue of outreach. If the Samaritan had given the injured man a tract of the five spiritual laws, he never would have reached the injured man's spiritual need. This man needed oil and wine poured on his wounds to cleanse them. He needed ambulatory care. He needed a place to rest and be healed, so the Samaritan took him to an inn.

When Jesus finished the story, he asked the lawyer, "Who was his neighbor?" But even after hearing the story, the lawyer was still entrenched in his racism and his distorted sense of cultural and religious superiority.

God's blessing came through the most unlikely channel. Imagine a pro-choice advocate helping a pro-lifer, or a Democrat helping a Republican. What would happen if an African American helped the grand dragon of the Ku Klux Klan, or a homosexual helped a homophobe? Imagine a Delta helping an AKA, or a Kappa helping an Omega. What would happen if an American Christian helped a member of Afghanistan's notorious Taliban?

Determination to demonstrate God's mercy as we go on our spiritual journey liberates us from ethnocentrism. It opens up the fact of the universality of God's love and that God is present in all people. God has many channels of blessing. If our family turns away and won't help, God has another channel of blessing. If our own people walk away, God has another channel of blessing. Through walking in mercy, both the giver and the receiver are blessed, and God is glorified.

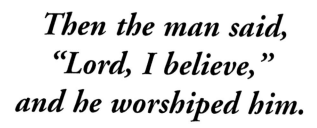

Then the man said,
"Lord, I believe,"
and he worshiped him.

John 9:38, NIV

ENLIGHTENMENT

John 9

After the blind man was healed, he not only gained his sight, but he gained enlightenment about the identity of the Messiah and was able to share that light with others.

Some years ago, the term lite became popularized, particularly among beer manufacturers. Lite beer was supposed to give drinkers all of the satisfaction of regular beer, without the calories. One popular slogan was "Tastes great, less-filling." Since that time, lite has crossed over to have other meanings, usually referring to anything that lacks substance or depth. The term has even made its way into religious faith because there are some believers who are lite Christians. They want all the joy of being a Christian, without being filled up. Believers who are filled up with the Holy Ghost are Christians of a different strand of the faith. We are light Christians— we who walk in the light of Jesus Christ filled with His spirit, receiving our direction from Him. We are the light of the world. But does our light shine so that the world can see us and thereby see Jesus?

There are a couple of times during the year when Christians everywhere have a platform to tell about Jesus. One of those days is Christmas, which is celebrated all over the world. Even people who do not believe in Jesus celebrate Christmas. Why? Because people like giving and receiving gifts; we like celebrating and spending time with friends and loved ones; we enjoy the special foods we eat only during that time of year. Yes, Christmas is a special holiday to the world. But without its counterpart, Christmas would have no real meaning. The fact that the Savior was born is complimented by the fact that He was crucified and rose from the dead. Christmas is good news of great joy, but Easter is shouting news. It is run-and-tell-everybody news.

Every Easter, over one billion people around the world celebrate the resurrection of our Savior. Whether Greek Orthodox, Baptist, Catholic, Presbyterian, Lutheran, or fire-baptized Holiness, we celebrate Resurrection Day. Whether in massive cathedrals, storefronts, or grass huts, on Easter morning believers around the world sing, "Christ the Lord is risen today!" How can an event that occurred over 2,000 years ago still have such a great impact on our world? Easter is the cornerstone of the Christian faith. But the life of Jesus Christ, from His birth to His resurrection, is the pivotal reference point for marking events in human history. Even atheists are impacted by the life of Jesus Christ. Every time we write a check, for example, we give unconscious acknowledgment to Jesus.

Any person who writes a date of the calendar year—whether that person is Christian, Muslim, Hindu, Buddhist, or New Age—acknowledges the life of Christ. A person who writes a check to pay taxes to the Internal Revenue Service may date the check April 15, 2003. Every year tallied since the reign of our Lord and Savior acknowledges Him. It was 1517 years after Christ that Martin Luther nailed his 95 Theses to the doors of the church. It was 1492 years after Christ that Columbus sailed the ocean blue. It was 1865 years after Christ that African Americans were emancipated from slavery. Our calendar is not determined by the life and ministry of Buddha, nor by that of Mohammed. Hare Krishna's reign is not reflected in each and every day of human history. No worldwide acknowledgment has endured regarding the existence of Confucius. No, the most significant event to affect human history is the birth, ministry, and resurrection of Jesus Christ. These events are even more important to the

Christian faith because we know that for over 2,000 years, Jesus has been reigning on a throne, not rotting in a tomb.

Jesus' resurrection validates His claims made in John 2:19. Furthermore, His resurrection verifies our continuation, as explained by the apostle Paul in 1 Corinthians 15:20: *But now is Christ risen from the dead, and become the firstfruits of them that slept. As Christ was raised from the dead, so shall all those who believe on His name. We don't like to talk about death, but the fact is that every person has a date with the dust, a date that cannot be canceled or postponed.* We are all going to die. A Gallup poll has indicated that one out of every one person is going to die in his or her lifetime. Each and every person will die unless the Lord tarries and doesn't come back to rapture us all.

A man had written on his tombstone, "As you are, so I once was. But as I am, so shall you be. So get yourself ready to follow me." Another man had etched on his tombstone, "To follow you I'm not content, until I know which way you went!" The good news for those who believe in Jesus Christ is that when we die, no one has to wonder which way we went. I'm going the same way that Jesus went! First Corinthians 15:20 tells us it is so for every believer.

An astute bystander can tell the difference between a believer and an unbeliever by going to a funeral. Unbelievers will fall out at a funeral because they don't have anything to look forward to after death. They will cry, try to stop the mortician from closing the casket, or

An astute bystander can tell the difference between a believer and an unbeliever by going to a funeral.

try to jump in the grave after the body. While children of God will mourn the death of loved ones, we have something to look forward to after death. At the cross, Jesus paid our sin debt. At the tomb, He gave all believers a receipt, one that guarantees that the debt has been paid in full. The resurrection of Jesus is our receipt that the gift of salvation cannot be taken away from us. Living, He loved us; dying, He saved us; buried, He carried our sins far away; rising, He justified us freely forever, and one day He is coming back. Oh, what a glorious day that will be!

The story is told of an elderly woman who told her pastor that she wanted to be buried with a fork in her hand. Intrigued by her unusual request, the pastor asked why. "Well, Pastor," she explained, "I've been to a lot of church dinners in my life, and the best dinners were those that, after they collected the plates, the servers said, 'Keep your fork.' When they told us to keep the fork I knew that something better was yet to come, like dessert. So when people look at my dead body holding that fork, they will know that the best for me is yet to come!"

All of the Gospel writers agree that Jesus was resurrected on the first day of the week. That is why Sunday is so important to Christians. All of the writers agree that He first appeared to the women who came to the tomb. There was a big stone at the entrance of the cave, which prevented grave robbers and animals from entering the tomb. He was heard to say, "It is finished," signaling that He voluntarily forfeited His life as a human being. What they don't agree on is the time that the resurrection actually took place. The Gospel of John says that Mary Magdalene went to the tomb while it was dark (20:1). Matthew 28:1 says as the dawn was just beginning. Mark 16:2 records the Resurrection occurring after the sun came up. These facts are not contradictory; they are complimentary. Each of them is giving an account of Mary Magdalene's journey to faith in the Resurrection. Together these three Gospel writers show the progress Mary Magdalene made toward the tomb. John picks her up as she commences her walk toward the tomb. When she started, John would say that it was dark. As she drew closer to the tomb, Matthew says it was beginning to dawn. By the time she arrived at the tomb, Mark tells us that a new day had begun. The closer Mary Magdalene came to the Resurrection, the closer she came to the light. By telling us about Mary's journey in stages, these three Gospel writers help us to understand that for every person, the farther we are away from Jesus, the more we are in darkness. The closer we get to Him, the more light we have in our own lives. Those who are living in darkness need to make their way to the Light of the World.

There are many kinds of darkness in our world—the darkness of secularism, which stubbornly refuses to acknowledge the sovereignty of God. There is the darkness that devalues human life so that the lives of far too many young African American men and women are cut short through acts of senseless gang and drug-related violence. Churches are afraid to hold funerals for deceased gang members because they fear an outbreak of violence in the church. There is the darkness through which a Trenchcoat Mafia is fashioned in suburban, middle-class Middle America. There is the darkness of nihilism, which leads to self-absorption. We have seen the results of the darkness of living in hopelessness and despair often touted in gangsta rap and certain elements of hip-hop culture.

The blind man in John 9 had lived in darkness all of his life, having been born blind. Jesus said, "I am the

There are many kinds of darkness in our world—the darkness of secularism, which stubbornly refuses to acknowledge the sovereignty of God.

Continuum of Our Relationship to Christ

Resistive (-6)
|
Retrospective (-5)
|
Seeker (-4)
|
Consideration (-3)
|
Revelation (-2)
|
Ready (-1)
|
Ground Zero (0)
|
Worship (1)
|
Water (2)
|
Work (3)
|
Witness (4)
|
Learner (5)
|
Well Done (6)

light of the world." After Jesus opened the man's eyes, he was continuously drawn closer to the Light. As the story progresses, each time the man explained his miraculous healing, he gave Jesus a different title. In verse 11, the newly sighted man refers to the Son of God as "the man called Jesus." By verse 17, the healed man was calling Jesus "a prophet." By verse 36, he knew Jesus as "Lord."

The Discipleship Continuum

Our relationship to Christ can be understood as a 13-stage continuum that draws us closer to Him. The first stage is minus six (-6), the Resistive stage. A person living in minus six is either resistant or nonchalant about the Good News. A resistant person wants nothing to do with Christ or His followers. If we are live according to our enlightenment in the knowledge of Jesus and not as a lite Christians, we have to be willing to seek out folks who are living at stage minus six.

Just above minus six, is the Retrospective stage. At minus five (-5), unsaved persons become aware of the void that is in their lives. That is when the difference between the Christians who are enlightened believers and lite Christians really becomes important. If a Retrospective person sees an enlightened Christian, the glow of that light may cause the person to become curious about the Source of that illumination. But if a Retrospective person sees a lite Christian, the opportunity for witnessing narrows because nothing special can be seen in a lite Christian.

Then comes minus four (-4), or the Seeker stage. At this stage, a person is asking the question, "What is the meaning of life?" and looking for answers. In the Consideration stage, minus three (-3), a person becomes open to looking at the church for answers to the question. At minus two (-2), the Revelation stage, the person begins to understand why he or she needs Christ. The last phase on the negative side of life is the Ready stage. At this stage, a person is ready to receive change.

Then there is the Ground Zero stage, when a person confesses Jesus Christ as Lord and Savior and begins new life in Christ. From the point of salvation, the person is ready for positive stage one (1), the Worship stage.

After the Worship stage is the Water stage (2), which is baptism—one's public acknowledgment of having accepted Jesus Christ as personal Lord and Savior. After baptism, we spend the bulk of our Christian journey in one of the next three stages. When the Work stage (3) begins it is because our orientation has changed and we begin to work for Him, not for ourselves. We move into the Witness stage (4) when we become more fully aware of what the Lord has done for us. It gets so good to us that we have to go out and tell somebody, anybody!

Stage five (5), Learner, is a constant state of learning and growing in Jesus Christ. And at the close of our earthly Christian walk is the Well Done stage (6), when we receive our admission ticket to our eternal home.

Then there is the Ground Zero stage, when a person confesses Jesus Christ as Lord and Savior and begins new life in Christ.

Servants for the Light (Matthew 5:14-16)

Jesus said to His disciples, "I am the Light." And He says to us today, "You are the light of the world." What He means is that all of His disciples are a continuation of what Jesus started in the world. We are now what He was then. He did not say, "You are the light of the church." So many Christians sit around church and congratulate each other because they are on their way to heaven, unlike the sinners who are scrambling around out in the world. We don't need light in the church. He wants us to be the light on our job. He wants us to be the light of our neighborhood. He wants us to be light in our household. He commands us to be the light of the world. The Christian community has tended to shun places and events that draw the children of darkness. But we, His light, are needed in those places. We are needed among those people. We have got to lift up Jesus. There is a lot of darkness in this world, so we, His light, have got to get busy!

Light Gives Direction

When we drive a car at night, the first thing we do after starting the engine is turn on the headlights. We can't maneuver without them. An airplane depends on runway lights to land safely and transport passengers to the proper terminal gate. The purpose of light is to banish darkness. The two cannot coexist. When light comes, darkness leaves. That is what Jesus does—He brings light to our lives and gives us direction. A whole lot of people are in trouble because they are getting direction from everywhere but On High. Some take direction of telephone psychics they see on television. Others look to friends for advice. But only Jesus Christ can give us the light we need to give us direction.

Conversely, Satan, the enemy, is known in the Bible as the Prince of Darkness. Therefore, a person is either pressing toward the Light or slipping into darkness. And the further we delve into the darkness, the harder it becomes to get out. There is an old saying, "Sin costs you

There is a lot of darkness in this world, so we, His light, have got to get busy!

more than you wanted to pay, takes you farther than you wanted to go, and keeps you longer than you wanted to stay." It is hard to pull away from addiction. It is hard to pull away from gossip. It is hard to walk away from adultery. It is hard to pull away from sin because Satan makes it easy to enter his world of darkness. He makes it feel comforting and cozy when we step in. But after we've been there for a while, and the farther we walk down the corridor of darkness, we notice a change. The dark place that seemed comforting when we stepped in has grown cold and discomforting. It is no longer soothing and inviting. And what's worse is that after we have gone in so deep, we can't find our way out. But that's what Satan wants us to think—that there's no way out of darkness. Lucifer rules the darkness, but thankfully, Jesus rules the light. It is only through Christ that we are able to find the way out of darkness. We need the light of Christ to give us direction.

There are people who seem to have everything that the world has to offer, but they are still in darkness.

The irony of this is that even those of us who live in the light still are not exempt from problems. But those of us who have the Light will make it through. There are people who seem to have everything that the world has to offer, but they are still in darkness. A child of darkness may live in a big house, but it is not a home, because there's no Light. A child of darkness may hold a fat bank account, but still be poor because of the darkness. A child of the dark is unable to see what is truly valuable in life. A child of the dark may drive an expensive car, but be lost because there is no Light to give direction. While some of those with worldly treasures stumble blindly in the dark, there are people who live without opulence, yet they live in the Light. There is no substitute for Jesus.

The Method of Shining—Good Works

There are two kinds of light—intrinsic light and reflective light. Jesus is intrinsic light. He is His own light source. He is self-generating light. We don't have to light Jesus; we just have to lift Him.

Christians are His light-bearers; we are reflective light. Our relationship to Him is like that of a light and its reflectors, like those found on bicycles, jogging shoes, or walkways. Reflective light cannot shine on its own power, it needs a source of light. When light hits reflectors, they shine. Their illumination is merely a reflection of the light that is shining on them. If we are aligned to Jesus, the intrinsic light will illuminate our reflection and we will begin to shine like never before. If we line up with Christ, His bright light will show up on us. When Moses came down from Mount Horeb, his face was shining because he had the glory of the Lord upon him. Our ancestors looked at that image and sang, "Shine on me, Lord. Let the light from the lighthouse shine on me."

Likewise, we have to encounter the Light—Jesus—so that we may reflect Him in our Christian walk. When others see our light shining, they get a glimpse of Him through us. When Jesus shines on us, nothing can put our light out. Even as our light shines we have to be careful because there are light-busters in the world. There are people in the world who do not want us to shine. So they talk about us to discourage us. They dig ditches for us to

Our relationship to Him is like that of a light and its reflectors, like those found on bicycles, jogging shoes, or walkways.

If we are to reflect His light, then it is time for some Christians to start getting crazy for Jesus.

try to make us fall in. They take advantage of our benevolence because they cannot stand the light of generosity. In spite of any obstacles, nobody can take away our Light if we shine for Jesus. We must remember that the world did many things to stop Jesus' light from shining. They crucified Him, trying to put His light out. They put Him in a tomb and closed it up, trying to put His light out. They guarded the tomb, trying to put His light out. But despite their best efforts, they could not put His light out because death could not keep Him in the grave.

If we are going to be the reflection of Jesus, then we need to think about some of the things that He did—like overturning the tables of the moneychangers—and emulate His actions. To the unbelievers at the Temple, He must have looked real crazy turning over those tables. If we are to reflect His light, then it is time for some Christians to start getting crazy for Jesus. We need to be crazy enough in Jesus to speak out to thug wanna-bes who disrespect our women, because Jesus respected all women. We need to be crazy enough to go out and reclaim our streets and our schools for Jesus. We need to be crazy enough to go out and feed some hungry folks and tell them about Jesus. We need to be crazy enough to help homeless folks find decent housing and let them know that He is the Light. I'm ready to come out of the closet for Jesus. Everybody else is coming out of the closet for what he or she claims is right. But what about Christians? Jesus said that nobody lights a candle to put it under a bushel (Matthew 5:15). We need to quit hiding our light in the closet. We put light up on a table so that we can let it shine. It is time for us to quit being

Sunday morning Christians and venture out into the world of darkness throughout the week. The time to let our light shine is when we leave church and go into the world.

Darkness is the absence of light. We don't walk into a room and turn on the darkness. Darkness cannot chase light away. When it gets dark every evening, it is not because darkness has chased the light away. It gets dark because the sun goes down. When the sun comes up again, the darkness flees. Light is invincible against the darkness. No one lights a candle and hides it; neither does God. We are His light, and He wants us to be visible.

Light is powerful and attractive, yet light does not draw attention to itself. Light does not shine for its own sake, but for the benefit of others. God does not equip us with spiritual gifts in order for us to be satisfied with ourselves. Rather, we are gifted so that we may benefit others by doing His will.

Therefore, since we are surrounded by such a great cloud of witnesses, let us throw off everything that hinders and the sin that so easily entangles, and let us run with perseverance the race marked out for us.

Hebrews 12:1, NIV

GRACE

Hebrews 11—12:2

The Bible records that as God's people journeyed with Him in faith, in both the Old Testament and the New, they experienced divine grace for the Christian journey.

The Word of God is the standard by which we determine truth and correct error. During the Reformation, this standard was termed *sola scriptura*, which means Scripture alone. Many people believe that the Holy Spirit will operate independent of Scripture. But the Holy Spirit, the Spirit of God, uses the Word of God to make the people of God like the Son of God.

Hebrews 11 is often deemed the hall of faith chapter of the Bible. It is the great faith chapter. The writer opens the eleventh chapter by defining faith as, "the substance of things hoped for, the evidence of things not seen."

Clarence Jordan is a great New Testament scholar who wrote a translation of the Scriptures known as the *Cotton Patch Version*. He translates Hebrews 11:1 this way: "Faith is turning dreams into deeds. Faith is betting your life on the unseen realities of God." Therefore, faith means betting our lives on the unseen realities of life. In other words, God has promised us things that we don't see, but faith says, "I'm gonna risk everything for that which I don't see." Believing God when we don't see the end result—that's faith.

After defining faith, the writer begins a roll call of persons who personify faith, who embody faith, or who bet their lives on the unseen realities of God. He mentions the faithful whom we recognize, such as Abraham, Moses, Abel, and Samson. But after offering these more familiar personalities who bet their lives on the unseen realities of God, the writer then lists a few "honorable mentions" from the hall of faith. These persons were less recognizable; nevertheless their lives yielded a great faith testimony. He closes the chapter by hailing the people who lived by faith while living in caves, who lived in faith even though they were destitute and had to wear sheepskin for clothing, and some who were mutilated.

After the hall of faith, the Hebrews writer uses the twelfth chapter to issue a challenge. It is a challenge borrowed from the wide world of sports. Hebrews 12:1 says, "*Wherefore seeing we also are compassed about with so great a cloud of witnesses, let us lay aside every weight, and the sin which doth so easily beset us, and let us run with patience the race that is set before us*" (KJV).

The first century A.D. was an era somewhat similar to the twenty-first century because they, too, were sports enthusiasts. They had their own kind of ESPN®, if you will. Because they loved sports so much, the New Testament writers used numerous sports analogies to explain the Christian life.

The beautiful thing about sports is that it can be good discipline, This benefit is made apparent in the statement, "Let us run with patience the race that is set before us." But that is not the only sports analogy found in the New Testament. First Corinthians 9:24-27 is replete with sports references. Paul asks, "Do you not know that in a race all the runners run, but only one gets the prize?" Here, he is making a reference to track and field. "But only one gets the prize" is a reference to competitive sports. Just like runners "run in such a way as to get the prize," Paul advises the Corinthians to do likewise in the

Christian race. Paul uses their understanding of a physical race to help them understand the nature of one that is spiritual.

In verse 25, Paul incorporates the importance of discipline in physical training to emphasize the importance of spiritual discipline, "Everyone who competes in the games goes into strict training. They do it to get a crown that will not last; but we do it to get a crown that will last forever." In Paul's day, after the race, the winner would go to a platform where the emperor would place a wreath on the victor's head. The wreath was a symbol of victory. The problem with this earthly symbol of victory is that eventually it would wither away. Paul advises the Corinthians to strive for the heavenly victory that will not wither or die. "Guess what?" he asks the Corinthians, "If you run your Christian race right, the God of the universe is going to place upon you a wreath that will not wither away." Paul explains in verse 26 that he runs with a purpose, not aimlessly.

Paul advises the Corinthians to strive for the heavenly victory that will not wither or die.

Finally, Paul presents another sports analogy, one that Mike Tyson could deal with. Paul compares himself to a boxer who does not waste his punches. First, he uses the example of a runner of track and field, then he gets into the boxing ring. If George Foreman, who is a devout Christian, had read that before his Rumble in the Jungle with Muhammad Ali in 1974, he wouldn't have lost his title. There in Zaire, Muhammad Ali employed his rope-a-dope style and out-strategized Foreman for the win.

Verse 27 is a rope-a-dope style verse. Paul explained, "I beat my body and make it my slave so that after I have preached to others, I myself will not be disqualified for the prize." As a spiritual athlete, Paul explained, "I've hardened my body with blows. I'm gonna get strong muscles, and lift weights. I'm going to bring my body under complete control to keep myself from being disqualified after I've called others to the contest."

Another sports analogy is Ephesians 6:12, using a different kind of sport. "For we wrestle not against flesh and blood, but against principalities, against powers; against the rulers of the darkness of this world, against spiritual wickedness in high places." One of the Greek words for strength is *stereo*, from which we get the word steroids. Christians are wrestling against demons, which means we cannot give up. We cannot lay down and give up when a problem comes along. Wrestling means saying to spiritual obstacles, "Come here, Demon! Come here, Liar! Come here, Depression! Come here, Crazy-maker! I'm not gonna quit! I'm gonna wrestle you down to the ground!"

Christians are wrestling against demons, which means we cannot give up. We cannot lay down and give up when a problem comes along.

The writer of Hebrews must have had in mind a vivid image of the great stadiums of Athens, Ephesus, Caeseara, and the Circus Maximus in Rome as he wrote the twelfth chapter. The massive Circus Maximus had a seating capacity of 180,000. People would come from all over the world to see their gladiators, runners, charioteers and other athletes compete. The Hebrews writer must have gone to Circus Maximus and seen the races. Perhaps he had watched the Pan-Ionian games in Ephesus. As he watched these games he probably had an awakening—there was something about these games that was similar to being a Christian. And so he said, "Wherefore seeing we are encompassed about with so great a cloud of witnesses." The writer issued an advisory that there is a great cloud of witnesses watching the Christian community; therefore, we must run the race that has been set before us.

Two preliminary observations are apparent in this text. The first is that we Christians are not as privileged as we think. When the writer of Hebrews needed an analogy to explain what it means to be a Christian, what did he use? Does he go to the corner where people are just chillin', trying to take it easy? Does he go to a retirement home? Or does he go to a stadium where there are runners exercising discipline in order to win a race?

Many Christians think that life will be easy for those who believe in Jesus. Christianity is a race. We are the Michael Jordans, the Evander Holyfields and the Serena Williamses who have to exercise all the discipline. An athlete like Evander Holyfield cannot be a champion without discipline. In fact, the word discipline describes the lifestyle to which we are called as Christians. The words disciple and discipline come from the same root. Just like an athlete has to discipline himself in order to win the prize, believers must exercise discipline in order to win the heavenly prize. Discipline is the capacity to refuse what we really want to accept. Discipline is the capacity to accept what we really want to refuse. Discipline is saying, "No, no, no!" when we truly want to say, "Yes, yes, yes!"

There are a whole lot of things that human beings can say "yes" to. The flesh says "yes," but discipline kicks in and says "no." Take, for example, a kid who is making A's in college, but he's away from home, away from his girlfriend, and can't find a girlfriend in college. He's tempted to leave school because his loneliness seems unbearable. But discipline says, "Even though I'm lonely, because I'm a disciplined man, I will stay here and stick it out."

Michael Jordan never would have become Air Jordan without discipline. And any Christian who has been successful in the Christian life has had to sacrifice, has had to say "no" to some things. Christians have to stay in spiritual shape. No believer can afford to think that being a Christian means coming to church and praising God, with no discipline in our daily living. Christians must have discipline with money, sex, our tongues, and with allowing other people to affect us. We are runners in the spiritual race. We are spiritual athletes.

As Americans, we are free to do just about anything we want. But for Christians this is not so.

Not only is the Christian life not as privileged because we are supposed to be disciplined, but the Christian life is not private. The text says we are "surrounded by a great cloud of witnesses." We are being observed. There is a great sea of faces. We don't even know they're watching. So it is naïve for a disciple of Jesus Christ to say "This is my life and it's nobody's business what I say or what I do." That is the most asinine statement a believer could ever make. Admittedly, each of us has been given a life to live, but folks make it their business to watch Christians. They are watching us when we praise God in the car, as we come to church, and as we interact in the community. They are watching how we behave under pressure. They are watching what we drink, how we treat our family, and how we conduct ourselves in the workplace. People are all over the place—watching. It is important how we carry ourselves because it can come back and haunt us. The Christian life is neither as privileged nor as private as our rights as Americans are. As Americans, we are free to do just about anything we want. But for Christians this is not so. We Christians must remember that we cannot slip and slide or dip and dodge, because somebody's watching. Paul says in 2 Corinthians 5:20 that we are ambassadors for Christ. We are His representatives in a world that is always watching.

That is why we must stay in shape. Yet, there are some spiritually flabby among His followers. Just like some people are physically flabby, there are believers who are not well toned spiritually. It doesn't take much to knock down a person who is spiritually out of shape. Getting in shape comes through prayer and fasting, Bible study and perseverance—refusing to give up when life gets tough. We will face opposition. Sometimes people will try to get in our way. Some people will try and prevent us from reaching our goal. That goes for goals in life as well as our heavenly goal. Sometimes it is the people closest to us who will say hurtful things in an attempt to destroy us or trip us up. We should not be surprised when it happens, because Jesus has already told us that these things will happen. Living amid such conditions means that we cannot afford to be spiritual chumps. The spiritually weak give up too quickly and spend too much time feeling sorry for themselves. Spiritual athletes keep going and going and going no matter what happens. When believers are spiritually strong, it doesn't deter them when people talk about them, lie on them, or try to abuse them. The eleventh chapter of Hebrews talks about the ex-athletes and other athletes who were sawed in half, lived in caves, were destitute, and had to wear sheepskin and goatskins. But they kept on going. Today, some people become discombobulated just because somebody doesn't speak to them!

When we know our race or our purpose, it reduces frustration. The last three words of Hebrews 12:1 "set before us" reveal the first thing we must do. The writer is using a sports analogy to explain that we believers must run the race that is set before us. That means we have purpose. Having purpose is essential because God has set before each of us a race that is different. The problem with many believers is that they are trying to run a race that God didn't give them. They are running a race that somebody else has assigned. But the key to being successful is knowing what race we are supposed to run. God has a race for every believer.

In Acts 20:24 Paul says, "But life is worth nothing unless I use it for doing the work assigned me by the Lord Jesus the work of telling others of God's mighty kindness and love." Notice, Paul emphasizes the work that was assigned to him, not someone else.

Each of us has an assigned work. We cannot let anyone else get us off of our purpose, track, or course, because a whole lot of people and elements are eager to create a course for someone who doesn't seem to have a purpose. Then that person will be running a race that God never intended. A whole lot of believers are frustrated because they don't know what their purpose is.

Running the right race increases our motivation. People tend to get motivated when they know they are running the right race. Running the right race allows for greater concentration. Every person can concentrate on his or her own race. They can "keep on keeping on."

Some believers right now are running and don't know how they're able to keep on running. They're tired. They've got obstacles in the way, but they keep on running. Other believers have to jump over some hurdles. Sometimes Christians have to jump over some things. Sometimes we are called to climb up the rough side of a mountain. But we are able to keep on because we have Jesus, who is the Finisher. He helps us finish. He helps us keep on going.

Running the right race prepares us for God's evaluation. God is going to evaluate each of us on the basis of our running the race that he gave us. I know what race I'm supposed to be running. God has appointed me to be a pastor/teacher and win people to Christ. He is going to evaluate me according to the race He chose for me. That's it.

Some people have said to me, "Cosby, you're supposed to be walking the streets." That's all well and good, but that's not my race. When we run the right race, we don't concern ourselves with what other people think. A whole lot of people are messed up because their lives are controlled by the opinions and approval of others. And until and unless we can mature in Christ to the point that we are running our own God-given race, we will always be influenced by the opinions of others, not God. Everybody is not going to pat us on the back or give us a sign of approval. Sometimes we have to win in opposition territory. Champions have to go for victory even when the crowd is hostile. Every game is not a home game with cheerleaders and mascots saying, "Go! Go! Go!" Sometimes we have to run past people who hate our guts.

Aerodynamic Christians

The word aerodynamic comes from two Greek words: *aerios*, concerning the air, and *dynamis*, meaning powerful. Aerodynamics is the study of forces and the resulting motion of objects through the air. All of our modern-day modes of transportation—planes, trains, and automobiles—are designed to be aerodynamic. They are designed to reduce drag against the wind and thereby increase their speed and fuel efficiency. Christians should be the same way in our spiritual walk. We should discipline ourselves to reduce the likelihood of people or circumstances dragging us down.

A whole lot of people are messed up because their lives are controlled by the opinions and approval of others.

The beginning of Hebrews 12 cautions us to "lay aside every weight, and the sin which doth so easily beset us." There are two things, then, that athletes have to get rid of. The first thing is excess weight. When Marion Jones is running, she doesn't wear a mink coat. There's nothing wrong with her wearing a mink, but Jones can't win if she is weighed down by an unnecessary fur coat. To be competitive, she strips down almost to indecency. Everything that could slow her down or impede her from running is laid aside. She must be aerodynamic when she runs.

If we want to win the race, we have to lay aside some things and possibly some people. The things we must lay aside are not necessarily bad, but they impede progress and slow us down. The things that weigh us down may be different for each of us. For me, one is the telephone. If it rings when I'm studying my Bible or preparing a sermon, it's a weight. There is nothing wrong with talking on the telephone, but when God wants me to prepare and preach, the phone becomes a weight I must lay aside because it is impeding me from doing my pastoral duties.

Some of us may have to lay aside the past and what people have said about us. Others may have to lay aside some friends. The friends may not be bad people, and they may even be Christians, but they are excess weight. Some people's weight may be an attitude or a bad habit. Whatever it is, only by laying that weight down can we be successful.

Weights and sins can so easily trip us up. When a runner puts on running shoes, he laces up each individual shoe. But no matter how great a runner he is, if he laces

If we want to win the race, we have to lay aside some things and possibly some people.

both shoes together, when they shoot the gun he's going to fall flat on his face. Running the race successfully means we must deal with sins that trip us up.

Sometimes laying aside the excess weight, just like losing weight, is difficult. It takes purpose, preparation, and perseverance. When the Hebrews writer says, "let us run with patience," that means perseverance. In other words, when we get in the race and the going gets tough, we keep going. We don't quit just because life gets hard. Perseverance is the Greek word *macrothermas*, which means "long heat." We have to be able to take the heat for long periods.

The kind of race mentioned in Hebrews is a relay race. We know it's a relay race because wherefore is a connecting word. The eleventh chapter deals with spiritual runners who had to run through all kinds of obstacles. They kept running until the "wherefore." Then Paul passes the baton to Timothy, who passes the baton to St. Augustine, who passes the baton to Frederick Douglass, who passes the baton to Sojourner Truth, who passes the baton to Martin Luther King, Jr., who passes the baton to Harold Ford, Jr., and so on. When the baton gets passed to us, it's time to run!

Every saint who passes the baton has run the race with perseverance. They have gone through all kinds of hell and all kinds of trouble along the race. They have sacrificed and served, only to hand the baton to the next generation of believers. The baton is in our hands today. But what happens if we fall while running with the baton? If we fall the past is disqualified and every sacrifice made to

Sometimes laying aside the excess weight, just like losing weight, is difficult. It takes purpose, preparation, and perseverance.

give us the baton is over. In the late 1950s and early 60s, Martin Luther King, Jr. was a fast runner. He took a bullet in the neck. People went to jail to give black folks the opportunities that we have right now. They suffered, they marched, and they sacrificed. My grandfather, B.J. Miller Sr., ran before me, serving as the pastor of St. Stephen Baptist Church for 44 years. He couldn't go to The Southern Baptist Theological Seminary because he was a black man. He had to stand in the hallways and listen to his professor's lecture. In spite of these obstacles, my grandfather graduated at the top of his class. He even had a scholarship named after him at Southern Seminary. So when he passed the baton to me, that means he's depending on me.

We should want to run the race the best we can because many people have sacrificed for us to get where we are.

We should want to run the race the best we can because many people have sacrificed for us to get where we are. A lot of black mothers have scrubbed somebody's floors and ironed somebody's clothes while they prayed for their children to be in the race. Our people cannot let those mothers down by acting stupid. If by our actions we disqualify the past, we also compromise the future. Some kids who want an opportunity to learn, grow, and gain exposure to larger, greater worlds may never be able to run. Our future as a people is in peril because we have a generation whose future is in jeopardy.

Finally, to run this race we need power. We can't run without power. And that is why we need grace for the race. Hebrews 12:2 tells about the power that keeps us going in the race. When we want to get tired, and the cramps start coming, and we want to give up and go home and sit down, Hebrews says, "Looking unto Jesus" who is first the author of our faith. In other words, He was the first runner. He is our example because Jesus has been running since eternity. He ran across the sky, hung the sun, ran and hung the moon, hung stars like chandeliers in the blue ether. He ran through 42 generations to Bethlehem, then after 30 years He ran to the Jordan and got baptized. As He ran, He healed the sick, cleansed the lepers, spread the good news of the kingdom from judgment hall to judgment hall, then ran down the Via Dolorosa to a place called Calvary and died. His journey didn't stop there. He ran into hell and preached a revival, and then early Sunday morning he ran back to the grave. He ran and declared all power. After 40 days He took a cloud and ran up to heaven where right now he's sitting at the right hand of the Father. He was the first, so that makes Him the Author.

One day He's going to run back and gather all the runners. That makes Him the Finisher. He will enable us to finish the race. We don't have enough strength to finish this race alone. There are too many obstacles. We need the Author and Finisher to win the race. We will finish the race because Jesus is the Finisher. When we want to give up, the Finisher picks us up and says, "Keep going." Isaiah 40:31 says, "They that wait upon the LORD shall renew their strength; they shall mount up with wings as eagles; they shall run, and not be weary; and they shall walk, and not faint."

The Author and Finisher of our faith gives us grace for the race. He gives us the power to keep on running.

*Then Peter began to speak:
"I now realize how true
it is that God does not
show favoritism."*

Acts 10:34, NIV

Diversity

Acts 10:34

As Peter grew in discipleship, he learned that God made all creatures and no one has the right to withhold the Good News from anyone else. Through divine revelation, Peter realized the joy of diversity.

An attorney was making his closing arguments before a jury in an attempt to exonerate his client. And as he passionately went about defending his client, he discovered that three jurors were missing from the jury box. And so the defense counsel stopped his presentation, looked at the judge and said, "Sir, I can't continue this because there are three jurors who are absent." And the judge said, "Don't worry, continue on. Yes, they are absent, but before they left they did give me their verdict." The three jurors had reached a verdict without waiting to hear all the facts.

On so many occasions, we are guilty of reaching verdicts about other people without knowing the facts. Sometimes we just hate people. We don't know why we hate them; we just don't like them. Perhaps there doesn't have to be a reason for disliking someone. All we know is that we just don't like them. But when a verdict about a person is reached without considering all the facts, we are engaging in sin. It is a form of sin that is tearing our world apart. It is the sin that is the root cause of the war in which America finds herself today — the sin of prejudice.

Prejudice occurs when we reach a verdict about someone without waiting to know all the facts. The word prejudice literally means to pre-judge or to make a judgment pre or before getting to know the person. To be prejudiced, or to make a pre-judgment about a person, is a terrible sin.

Prejudging others is sin because God doesn't operate like that. When God sent Samuel to anoint a king to succeed Saul, He said, "Don't look at the outward appearance," because human beings look at the outward appearance. The Lord said, "But I look at a person's heart." And God does. God is not concerned with the superficialities of skin tone, physical size, socioeconomic status, or academic accomplishment. God is not concerned with zip codes or geographic regions. God is concerned with one thing — that is the heart of a person.

God is not only concerned with the heart of people but God is also concerned with trying to move the church toward being concerned with what He's concerned about. If God is not concerned with color, we shouldn't be concerned with color either. Since God only judges the heart — we should only judge the heart. And the Lord is trying to move us in that direction.

As we grow in grace, we move beyond our prejudices. And just because we're saved, doesn't mean we're not prejudiced. Christendom has a lot of saved, prejudiced folk within its ranks. That's not in God's will and it's certainly not God's will for our lives, but it's possible to be saved, it's even possible to be a preacher or an apostle, and still be prejudiced.

We need look no further than the apostle Peter, who was a gracious man. He was a very, very prejudiced man. Once the Lord tried to get Peter to witness to a man from a different culture. He prepared Peter by lowering a sheet down while Peter was asleep on a rooftop. And on that sheet were various animals that Jews were prohibited from eating. On this sheet were the African American equivalent to pig feet, chitterlings, and barbecued ribs with cole slaw and corn bread. God was not trying to move Peter to change his diet, but to change his disposition about people who did eat that kind of food.

The text says that Peter looked at the Lord and said, "Lord, I'm not going to eat that food. I'm a Jew and Jews don't eat that stuff." And God said to Peter, "Don't you call unclean anything or anyone whom I have declared to be clean." God had to force a reluctant Peter to move beyond his prejudice about non-Jews. Peter had been walking with the Lord for a while and now it was time to go further. As he went on his journey with the Lord, Peter began to move beyond prejudice and racism in the name of religion. Sometimes God has to force His people to do something. He may force us to love somebody. He had to force Peter into going to Caesarea to witness to one Cornelius, an Italian. Cornelius was a Roman soldier, a centurion. God moved Peter to travel 32 miles. The Lord grabbed him and Peter responded, "I won't go. I don't like those kinds of people. I don't like those Italians. I'm a Jew. I only witness to Jews. I only preach to Jews. I only want to benefit Jews." Peter was explaining his prejudicial stance to the Lord as if He did not understand. And really, He doesn't. Because God loves every human being equally so it must not make sense to Him.

Peter finally got to Caesarea and met Cornelius, who had been praying for revelation on how he might be saved. Peter was preaching to Cornelius and in the midst of preaching the Holy Spirit fell on Cornelius. And Cornelius, an Italian, was filled with the Holy Spirit just like Peter, a Jew, was filled with the Holy Spirit.

As he went on his journey with the Lord, Peter began to move beyond prejudice and racism in the name of religion.

And the text says that Peter knew that Cornelius was filled with the Holy Spirit because he started speaking in tongues and praising God. This shocked Peter. In that instant, Peter had a paradigm shift. In his previous paradigm, the only people who could be filled with the Holy Spirit were Jews. In Peter's limited scope, the only people who could praise God were Jews. According to the text, Peter opened his mouth and said, "of the truth, I perceive." Any time we receive new revelation or insight, we experience a paradigm shift. He said, "I perceive that God is no respecter of persons." That is to say that while people look at other people based on external factors such as race, God doesn't. If He did, He wouldn't be filling believers of every race, color, and creed with His Holy Spirit.

God is no respecter of persons. He created human diversity with intentionality and purpose. God is not prejudiced. Prejudice is a sin. Therefore, prejudice is not found in God because sin is not found in God. White folk may not like black folk. Serbs may not like Croatians. Palestinians may not like Jews or vice versa. A Hindu may not like Muslims or a Muslim may not like Hindus. A poor Hispanic may not like an affluent Hispanic. A Black Nationalist may not like Bubba, a tobacco-chewing redneck. Just because the Black Nationalist doesn't like Bubba, doesn't mean God doesn't like Bubba because God is no respecter of persons.

Unfortunately, although God is no respecter of persons, His people place value judgments on each other all the time. In the church, a congregation of one race may accept persons from different races, but they can't rise too high in the hierarchy in the leadership ranks. For instance, a black person can't be chair of the deacon board at a white church. Or a white minister of music can't get hired at a black church. But when we make such determinations, we must remember that the church we attend is not our church; its God's church.

Christians tend to regard some sins as felonies and other sins as misdemeanors. For instance, a man sleeping with another man's wife is a felony. But not speaking to a person of a different race is a misdemeanor. Some Christians console themselves in their prejudice, believing, "You're gay, and that's a felony. But if I don't like white people, that's only a misdemeanor. But prejudice and racism are not misdemeanors because there are no misdemeanor sins. Harboring the feelings that breed racial strife is no minor sin.

Prejudice says, "God accepts me because of race... or because I'm black or I'm white. God accepts me because I'm a brother or because I'm fine. But being black won't get a person into heaven. You can be deceived in your blackness. Wearing kufis and kenté cloth made in Taiwan will not earn a black person a ticket into heaven. In heaven, the key is not race, but grace. We don't get to heaven because of race. We sing "Amazing Grace," not "Amazing Race." Grace gets us into heaven. And God gives grace to all people because He's no respecter of persons. He gave grace to Peter, a Jew. And He gave grace to Cornelius, an Italian.

There's a story about a man who dreamed that he had died and was at the gate of hell. The man asked the gatekeeper if there were any blacks there. The gatekeeper said, "Yes." The man asked, "Well, are there any whites in there?" The gatekeeper looked at him and said, "Yeah." And then the man asked, "Well, are there any Hispanics or Asians in hell?" And the gatekeeper looked in and said, "Yeah." Then the man had a dream that he went to heaven. And he peeked inside the pearly gates asked Saint

In heaven, the key is not race, but grace. We don't get to heaven because of race.

Peter, "Are there any blacks in heaven?" Saint Peter said, "No." He said, "Well, are there any whites in heaven?" Saint Peter again said, "No." "What about Orientals and Hispanics?" Once more, Saint Peter answered "No." Curious, the man then asked, "Well, who's in there then?" And Saint Peter explained, " There are no races here, only children of God."

Acts 17:26 says, *He hath made of one blood all nations of men.* God made all human beings of one blood. God made all nations from one blood. God made black folk from one blood and from that same blood made white folk and Hispanic folk and Asian folk. Therefore, if God made all nations from one blood, that means people who have a problem with cultural or ethnic diversity need to take it up with God! Furthermore, it means that no nation is culturally deficient. Different does not mean to be deficient.

So that means if God made all nations of one blood, white folks like Bubba, who listen to Hank Williams Jr., sing "Your Cheating Heart," are all right. From one blood means that it's okay to be Latino and living la vida loca. Conversely, African Americans need not be ashamed of the way God made us. God made black people on purpose. If a black man or woman is ashamed of certain aspects of blackness, then that person is saying that God, in creating black people, is guilty of creative malfeasance.

God didn't make a mistake in making big, full brown noses, full figures, big lips, and big behinds. That says Patti LaBelle doesn't have to trim down her nose.

If a black man or woman is ashamed of certain aspects of blackness, then that person is saying that God, in creating black people, is guilty of creative malfeasance.

Michael Jackson doesn't have to do anything to his skin. There was a time when some black folks talked about, "good hair" or "bad hair." Words like good and bad are adjectives that offer value judgments. Hair, in and of itself, is neither good nor bad. Hair is incapable or possessing moral qualities. Any hair that covers the head—even if it's a weave,—is good hair!

The diversity of human features means that our God is creative. God likes diversity and has given to all races and cultures equally. The Holy Ghost filled Peter the Jew as well as Cornelius the Italian, because God is the Author of diversity. And for those who think that the only people in the Bible are Jews and Italian Europeans, black folk are represented in the Bible, too—next to whites; next to Jews. Contrary to what those in the Nation of Islam and the Seven Percenters—who said that the Bible is a white man's book packed to propagandize and brainwash black folk—would have us believe, black folks are all through the Bible.

The problem is that too many folks have been watching Cecil B. DeMille's "Ten Commandments," rather than reading their Bibles. They think Moses looked like Charlton Heston and Miriam looked like Vivian Leigh. But look at the record. Numbers 12;1 reads, *Miriam and Aaron spake against Moses because of the Ethiopian woman whom he had married.* Moses had a sista for a wife. Moses married a black woman, which means there was interracial marriage in the Bible. Moses' sister Miriam got upset because Moses married outside of his race. Then God got upset because Miriam got upset that her brother married outside the race. And God turned Miriam into a leper because of her racism.

Now, suppose God turned all people into lepers who didn't like interracial marriage! Young David, who slew Goliath, had a wife by the name of Bathsheba. The word *Bath* is Hebrew for daughter. Sheba is an African country. So, that means Bathsheba was a daughter of Africa. In Song of Solomon 1:5, Solomon's wife is talking to him. She describes herself as, "black but comely." And Solomon was the wisest man in the world. Somebody said the reason why he was so wise was because he had a sister, a black woman, for a wife.

Moses, David, and Solomon—three of the greatest men in the Bible—were in interracial marriages and God didn't get upset. He didn't get upset because God is no respecter of persons. In the New Testament we find racial and cultural diversity as well. The first church, the Jerusalem Church, was an interracial congregation. And the first problem in the first church was an interracial problem—the Greeks were grumbling because their widows were not being cared for in the same manner as the Hebrew-speaking widows (Acts 6:1). There was systemic racism in the Jerusalem Church, and it manifested itself in the food distribution, which necessitated the call of deacons.

There was systemic racism in the Jerusalem Church, and it manifested itself in the food distribution, which necessitated the call of deacons.

In the Gospels, when Jesus was carrying His cross and he couldn't carry the weight of the cross alone, the Bible says they got a black man to help Him, Simon of Cyrene, which is in northern Africa. So in the Bible all believers—whether African, European, Jewish, or Palestinian—were all filled with the Holy Ghost. We all are saved by the same blood and we are all going to the same heaven.

So since we all have this commonality in the body of Christ, there need not be any prejudice. One Sunday at our church, a white preacher delivered the message. When he got up some folk wanted to leave. But after he started preaching about the fishes and the loaves, they decided to stay a while. After the service was over, the tape was selling like hotcakes. When the Holy Ghost comes on us—and He is no respecter of persons—whether black, white, red, brown, female, or male, it's intoxicating. When the Holy Ghost came at Pentecost, observers said, "They must be drunk." Peter told them, "No, the bars are not open yet. These people are not drunk; they're intoxicated with the Holy Ghost." What they experienced that day was the fulfillment of what God spoke through the prophet Joel in the Book of Joel 2:28. "I will pour out my spirit upon all flesh. Your sons and your daughters shall prophesy. And that's what he's doing. God is pouring out His Spirit on all flesh, black flesh, red flesh, white flesh, brown flesh, yellow flesh, male flesh, and female flesh.

The Test

Given the fact that racial diversity is affirmed repeatedly in the Bible as an intentional act of God, how can we be content in our prejudices? We need to examine ourselves and ask, Am I a Miriam? Am I an Aaron? We need to look for the ways we try to annihilate human diversity instead of celebrating God's creative handiwork.

The Travesty

Every one of us receives grace. We're in church because of grace. So, how can we who receive grace not give grace to somebody else? How can any of us be xenophobic—hate folks who are different—when each of us has been saved by a foreigner? How can we hate foreigners when it was a "foreigner" who gave His life for our salvation? Jesus was no auburn-haired, European-looking brother. Jesus looked more like

Osama bin Laden than Leonardo da Vinci's Jesus in "The Last Supper." So, that means every time a Christian racially profiles an Arab, that person is saying "I can't like you, Jesus," because Jesus looked just like an Arab. Most of the world's Christians have been saved by a Person from a different race. So how can we be racist? Most Christians are not Jews, and Jesus was a Jew.

There is a story about something that happened when Hitler ruled Germany. He had issued an edict that all Jews who converted to Christianity had to leave the church. One Sunday, after a German soldier read the edict in a Lutheran church, each one of the Jews started to leave. Suddenly, they heard the sound of something being unscrewed. When they looked up, they noticed the sound was coming from a crucifix located in the back of the church. When the soldier ordered all Jews to get out, Jesus started taking the screws out of his hands, pulling the nails from His feet. He was preparing to walk out with the rest of the Jews because He, too, was a Jew.

God can bring us together, but there's got to be some repentance.

The Truth

God can bring us together, but there's got to be some repentance. Black folks have to repent from thinking that all white folks are evil. We also have to quit thinking that all black folks are our brothers and sister. We must quit blaming white racism for black irresponsibility.

White folks have to repent. White folk have to admit that the only reason there's racism in America is because Christians have perpetrated it. They have to admit that America is not this beautiful great nation that we love to sing about. America is a nation that was founded on theft and injustice—with land that was stolen from Native Americans and built with the labor of black folk forced into slavery.

The Southern Baptist Convention, the nation's largest Protestant denomination, came into existence because of racism. In 1845, white Baptists in the slaveholding South split from northern white Baptists. Northern Baptists had begun to question whether slavery was wrong. They rightfully questioned how a slaveholding, southern Christian could be commissioned as a missionary to go and spread the Gospel in foreign lands, to people of color, no less. But southern Christians were firm in their belief that black folks should be slaves.

Although they were not slaveholders, racism was a core issue among northern Christians as well. The historic Abyssinian Baptist Church in New York City was founded because of racism. In 1808, a group of traders from Abyssinia, better known today as Ethiopia, attended the First Baptist Church of New York. They resented being escorted to the slave loft and promptly walked out in protest. A short time later the protesters purchased property and established Abyssinian Baptist Church.

The African Methodist Episcopal Church and the AME Zion Church were formed in response to racism. Richard Allen started the AME Church and John Varrick started the AME Zion Church because whites in the Methodist Church would not let black folks come to the altar.

Prejudice and racism also factor prominently in the Church of God in Christ. Dr. Seymour, a black man founded the COGIC denomination because, although black and white folks alike had gotten filled with the Holy Ghost on Azusa Street, the whites didn't want the leader of their church to be a black man, so they established the Assemblies of God.

So how can we expect Serbs and Croatians to get together? How can we expect Catholics and Protestants to get together? How can we expect Palestinians and Jews to get together? How can we expect the world to get together if the Church won't get together? If we are to change the world then we must start inside the Church. God tells us in His Word that *If my people which are called by my name will humble themselves, pray, seek my face, I will heal the land* (2 Chronicles 7:14, KJV).

If we are to change the world then we must start inside the Church.

That means Christians ought to go out of our way to make friends with somebody of a different race. We sponsor a monthly men's breakfast at St. Stephen. The men's breakfast has always been an interracial event. We have white brothers who come over and fellowship with us at the men's breakfast. But the only problem in the beginning was that while it was well attended, blacks were always sitting at one table, and whites were always sitting at another. One Saturday I was late getting to the breakfast. And as I normally do, I went to sit next to my (black) friends. But all the chairs at the table were full. Every chair at every table was full, except one—a table with all whites. I kept looking around but there wasn't a seat anywhere, except at the white table. I looked for some extra chairs, but there were no extra chairs anywhere. In retrospect, I realized that the Lord was setting me up. The Lord arranged it so there would be no chairs, because I can't very well talk about racial harmony to the congregation if I don't practice it first. The Lord said to me, "Sit down, Boy." After I sat down a white man said, "Kevin, I'm glad you're sitting next to me. I had a tape made for you. Here it is." Then another white man said, "Kevin, here's a book I brought it for you. I got it autographed. Here, I want you to have it." Then another white man said, "I just got through writing a book. This is your copy I want you to have it." Now when I sit at the black table, none of those Negroes gave me a thing! That day the Lord affirmed something I needed to be reminded of—we never know who God is going to use to bless us.

When we are willing to stretch ourselves beyond our small zones of racial and cultural comfort, the Lord has a blessing in store for us.

Christians have to be different. We can't make a difference in the world if we ourselves are not different. We have to set the example. Other folks might judge on the basis of color, but Christians must judge on the basis of salvation. Other folks may look on outward appearances, but Christians must look in the heart. If the world is going to change, the church has to change first. Preachers have to change. Choirs have to change. Deacons have to change. Congregations have to change. Ushers have to change. That's a total and complete change.

Repentance means turning around a full 180 degrees. We can't live for race one minute and grace the next. The Bible says that judgment must begin in the house of the Lord. We have to repent without worrying about being persecuted by people who don't understand or who are unwilling to change. The children of God can't worry about that. We live for an audience of One. We're trying to please Jesus.

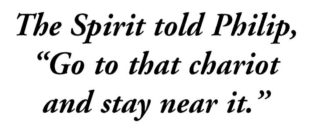

*The Spirit told Philip,
"Go to that chariot
and stay near it."*

Acts 8:29, NIV

EvANGElism

As Philip journeyed in Christ, he experienced the fulfillment of evangelism—telling someone about the saving power of Jesus Christ and leading them to make a decision for Him.

The primary purpose of the Church is winning the lost to Christ and helping them to grow in their faith and become responsible members of Christ's church. Within the Church we have two models of evangelism: personal and mass. Both can be illustrated by Jesus' metaphor: "Follow me and I will make you fishers of men." Two different models of fishing can be found in the New Testament: net fishing and line fishing—casting a net or casting a line. Net fishing is when you catch a lot of fish—dragnet, like the methods used by the Reverend Billy Graham or Bishop T.D. Jakes. Line fishing is when you catch just one person.

In Jesus' statement He defines what His followers do. Jesus' followers fish. Jesus was saying, "If you are following Me you will be fishers of lost people." For example, at the beginning of Jesus' ministry (Luke 5:4), He told Simon to launch out to the deep and lower his net. By the close of His earthly ministry in John 21:5-6, the disciples had been fishing all night and had caught nothing. The resurrected Christ told them to cast their nets on the right (opposite) side. They obeyed Jesus and caught so many fish that they couldn't draw in the net.

At the beginning and at the conclusion of Peter's ministry he was engaged in net fishing. This is the kind of fishing that occurs on

Sunday morning when we extend an invitation to discipleship. Matthew 17:27 contains an example of line fishing...you just catch one. The disciples needed to pay their taxes and the Lord told Peter to go to the sea and cast a line and catch a fish. Inside the fish Peter would find a piece of money—enough to pay the taxes!

Philip must have been thinking, "We have perfected the art of net fishing. It's safe. It's less intimidating, and more prestigious." The net fishing style of personal evangelism is vital to the growth of the Kingdom. Philip engaged in both types of fishing. Philip had been successful in Samaria net fishing. But the Lord sent him to Gaza to do line fishing.

Who was this fisherman named Philip? He was one of the seven chosen to help the apostles in the administration of the church. The Bible describes him as a man of wisdom, honest report, and full of Holy Spirit. The description, "full of Holy Spirit" means that he had postured his life so that there was no room for anyone else. Since Philip was filled with God he had no room for anything but God. The human heart has the capacity to be filled with many things, just ask Legion. All kinds of demons can tempt us and torment us. A man who can't seem to control his desire for women is filled with lust—and his lust comes before God. A person consumed with more money, more power, or even more food puts greed before God. The woman who looks at people solely for what she can take, steal, or con from them is with larceny, and it has moved ahead of God in terms of her priorities. Human beings can allow practically anything to come between them and God—rage, covetousness, jeal-

A person consumed with more money, more power, or even more food puts greed before God.

ousy/envy, or even ambition.

Philip was full of the Holy Spirit. To be full of the Holy Spirit means to be controlled. The word picture of what it means to be controlled is that of a ship with sails open and filled with wind. The wind causes the sail drives the ship in the direction that the wind wants it to go. The fact that Philip was filled with the Spirit does not mean that he engaged in bizarre or extreme behavior. It does not mean that he was a candidate for an episode of the "X-Files." It does not mean he was weird. The description of Philip as a man filled with the Holy Spirit means that he relied on God to direct his life. A prime example of this is Acts 8:26. In that passage an angel told Philip where to go to a desert road toward Gaza. The verse tells us what he is being driven to, and what he is being driven from. Desert road-barren, hostile. Sometimes people feel like the road of life is barren for them. They feel like no one cares. Some may even feel as though life holds no meaning for them. Our Christian call to evangelism calls us to venture down desolate roads in search of such people.

Our Christian call to evangelism calls us to venture down desolate roads in search of such people.

But what really demonstrates that Philip is controlled by God is evidenced in what he is being driven from. We are told in Acts 8 that Philip was pastor of a vibrant church in a city in Samaria. It is a church that is receptive to his ministry. In Acts 8:5, Philip went down to a city in Samaria and proclaimed the Christ there. Acts 8:6: When the crowds heard Philip and saw the miraculous signs he did, they all paid close attention to what he said.

The people were paying attention to the Gospel. There was healing and deliverance. So successful was his ministry that Peter and John came to investigate—which resulted in the Samaritan Pentecost. At the height of this revival and Philip's success, an angel of the Lord said, "Go to the desert."

Sometimes God moves us from a ministry because we have lost vision. Sometimes God moves us because people are not receptive to the vision. They put up "do not disturb" signs on the church. When ministers experience unreceptive people, Jesus' example teaches us to shake the dust off our feet and move on. Philip has none of these problems. God led him away from his ministry for a different reason. God will drive us to another assignment when He is moving us to a higher calling. A higher calling does not necessarily mean a bigger and more prestigious place.

God will drive us to another assignment when He is moving us to a higher calling.

In Phil 3:14, Paul says "I'm pressing toward the mark of the high calling." He wrote that from jail. Pressing on to a high calling does not necessarily mean a bigger building, a larger salary, or more prestige or political clout. That's hard for us to recognize in our society, which places such a premium on our "bigness." Our society says you're not successful if you're not visible. How could going to Gaza in the desert be a higher calling? How could preaching to one man...one black man...be more beneficial than leading a whole city in a revival? It's what Martin Luther King, Jr. did when he went to the garbage collectors in Memphis shortly before his death.

My friend and colleague Dr. Bruce Williams, pastor of Bates Memorial Baptist Church in Louisville, Kentucky, is one of the most powerful preachers in America. He has been invited to pastor some of the largest churches in America. Everyone has encouraged him to leave the poor neighborhood called Smoketown where Bates Memorial is located because of the drugs, alcohol, rampant poverty, illiteracy, and proliferation of single parents. His response is "The reasons why people say I should leave are the exact reasons why I need to stay." Dr. Williams can pastor a bigger church, but he won't necessarily receive a higher calling.

How do we know that Philip received a higher calling? Notice Philip's response. He is filled with the Holy Spirit. So he started out. He didn't know why he was going. He was full of the Spirit, on his way he met an Ethiopian eunuch. The Ethiopian Eunuch was a God-fearer because he had been to Jerusalem. God fearers were Gentiles who accepted the ethics of Judaism, the monotheism and the ethics of Judaism, but for some reason could not convert. The reason he could not convert was because of Deuteronomy 23:1, *No one who has been emasculated by crushing or cutting may enter the assembly of the Lord* (NIV).

He had gone to worship, but left disappointed. How many people leave church disappointed? He came seeking bread, but left hungry. He came seeking water, but left thirsty. He came seeking fellowship, and left lonely. He came seeking hope, but left despondent. The text says he has possessions—he had a chariot and he had a position of authority. He was the treasurer to Queen Candace. He had prestige and great authority, but he had a problem. God called Philip from net evangelism to casting a line and he's walking by the chariot.

Philip asks the man if he knows what he is reading. The Ethiopian official invites Philip to join him. Philip is invited. That says something about evangelism. The Holy Spirit has to prepare and get the seeker ready to hear the Good News. In verse 35, Philip began with the very passionate passage talking about Jesus Christ. The point of the text is Christ. The question is asked, how many gospels are there in the Bible? We say four, but the truth is there are 66. All of the Gospels, all of the Old Testament, all passages of the Bible point to Christ. There was no New Testament during the walk to Emmaus (Luke 24:27). In John 5:39, Jesus said to the Pharisees, "Search the scriptures; for in them you think you have eternal life. But these are they that testify of me." That means the Bible is one book with one Author and one coherent message—and that message is Christ. Whether we are preaching from the Law, the Prophets, the historical books, Wisdom Literature, Gospels, the Epistles, or the Apocalypse, they all relate directly to Jesus.

We can never know where God's call is going to lead us and what the results will be.

Philip and the official came to some water and the eunuch said, "Stop the chariot. What is hindering me from being baptized?" When Christ comes in, we want to stop certain things. The chariot was a symbol of the eunuch's prestige and power, but he said "Stop that." When Christ comes in, everything stops. There's no need to try and impress people. After the Ethiopian official was baptized he went away rejoicing.

If we follow Him in faithful obedience, however, we will yield unimaginable results. A story that has circulated the Information Superhighway illustrates my point.

A man was sleeping one night when suddenly his room filled with light and the Savior appeared. The Lord told the man He had work for him to do. He and showed the man a large rock in front of his cabin. The Lord told the man to push against the rock with all his might. This the man did, day after day. For many years he toiled from sun up to sun down, his shoulders set squarely against the cold, massive surface of the unmoving rock, pushing with all his might. Each night the man returned to his cabin sore, and worn out, feeling that his whole day had been spent in vain. Since the man was showing signs of discouragement, the Adversary decided to enter the picture by placing thoughts into the man's weary mind: "You have been pushing against that rock for a long time, and it hasn't budged. Why kill yourself over this? You are never going to move it." Thus, giving the man the impression that the task was impossible and that he was a failure. These thoughts discouraged and disheartened the man. "Why kill myself over this?" he thought. "I'll just put in my time, giving just the minimum effort, and that will be good enough." And that is what he planned to do, until he decided to make it a matter of prayer and take his troubled thoughts to the Lord. "Lord," he said, "I have labored long and hard in your service, putting all my strength to do that which you have asked. Yet, after all this time, I have not even budged that rock by half a millimeter. What is wrong? Why am I failing?" The Lord responded compassionately, "My friend, when I asked you to serve me and you accepted, told you that your task was to push against the rock with all your strength, which you have done. Never once did I mention to you that I expected you to move the rock. Your task was to push. And now you come to me with your strength spent, thinking that you have failed. But is that really so? Look at yourself. Your arms are strong and muscled. Your back is sinewy and brown. Your hands are callused from constant pressure, and your legs have become massive and hard. Through opposition you have grown much and your abilities now surpass that which you used to have. Yes, you haven't moved the rock. But your calling was to be obedient and push to exercise your faith and trust in My wisdom. This you have done. I, my friend, will now move the rock."

At times God calls us to do things for Him that we can't fully comprehend. If we are desire to render faithful service to Him, we cannot rely on our own understand. God wants faithfulness and obedience, not understanding.

Why would God interrupt a thriving revival in a city to send Philip to win one man in the desert? Because history tells us that this Ethiopian is the father of the African Coptic church. That means that the Gospel, for the first time, moved into the interior of Africa— Ghana, Songhay, Timbuktu, all because Philip obeyed the Lord and ventured down that desolate road. He didn't realize it when he responded to God, but Philip went from reaching a city in Samaria, to reaching an entire continent—Africa.

Epilogue

For many years, Western Europe believed the world ended at the eastern end of the Strait of Gibraltar—what is called the Pillars of Hercules. On the old Mideval maps, ancient mapmakers would write across the Strait of Gibraltar the Latin phrase *ne plus ultra*, which means "no more beyond." Then, in 1492, a Genovese sailor named Christopher Columbus discovered new territory, the New World. The old maps had to be revised and the words *ne plus ultra* were replaced with *plus ultra*, "more beyond."

Many people have put on the maps of their lives *ne plus ultra*. They believe there's nothing beyond divorce, disappointment, abuse, or other apparent life failures. But Christ has come to revise the maps of our lives so that we can write *plus ultra*—more beyond—on the scroll of our hearts. We have explored how many of the Bible characters were able to revise the maps of their lives.

Like the ten lepers mentioned in the Introduction of this book, who society said there was nothing beyond their painful predicament, but they cried out, "Jesus, Son of David, have mercy on us, and discovered that there was much more beyond—*plus ultra*—as they went.

What is essential for any life to move beyond tragedy is radical faith. Faith is more than believing in God. Faith is believing God. We often think that we have to see it to believe it. But the opposite is true. We have to believe it before we can see it. The ten lepers believed before they saw their healing.

Leviticus 14:1-9 gives detailed instructions on how the healing of lepers is to be verified so that they could reenter society, beginning with the priest going outside the camp to the diseased person. That would prevent the infection of others in case the person was not actually healed. But the ten lepers did not do that. They took a risk and went directly into the city. But because they were willing to go beyond the religious regulations and obey Christ, they were healed. Christ put people above policies. Had they stayed with the policies, they could not have uttered, "*plus ultra.*"

But because they were willing to go beyond the religious regulations and obey Christ, they were healed.

We live in a safety driven society that discourages risk-taking. We have OSHA, the Food and Drug Administration, Housing Inspection and Codes agencies. Imagine if Noah had built the ark in our day. He probably couldn't get a construction permit. OSHA would shut him down because they were no fire extinguishers or flotation devices. He would be cited by the city for violating zoning laws. The environmentalists would protest Noah for cutting down Gopher wood. The army corps of Engineers would be critical of Noah's unacceptable flood plan. And the ACLU would take him to court because he said that God told him to do it, which makes it unconstitutional.

But faith means obeying God. Martin Luther said "We are not saved by faith and works." But we are saved by faith that works." That is why to know the will of God is the greatest knowledge. To find the will of God is the greatest discovery. And to obey the will of God is the greatest achievement.

There is such a gap between our theology and our reality in the Christian community. We talk about how great and powerful God is. But when it comes to taking risks in obedience, as the ten lepers did, we remain outside the city gates.

Only as we are able to rise above our fears and obey the lead of God in our lives will we find ourselves becoming the people whom God is calling us to be. As they went they were healed...and then *plus ultra*.

Works Cited

Alcott, Louisa May. *Little Women*, was originally published in 1868-69 by Little, Brown and Company

Bach, Richard, *Jonathan Livingston Seagull.* New York: Macmillan and Sons, 1970.

Buchanan, Mark. *Your God Is Too Safe.* Sisters, Oregon: Multnomah Publishers, 2001

Jordan, Clarence. *The Cottonpatch Version of Paul's Epistles.* New York: Association Press, 1968.

Keller, Timothy J. *Ministries of Mercy: The Call of the Jericho Road.* Phillipsburg, New Jersey: Presbyterian & Reformed Publishing Company, 1997

Larsen, Bruce *There's a Lot More to Health than Not Being Sick* (W Publishing Group, 1984).

ABOUT THE AUTHOR

Kevin W. Cosby, D.Min.

F ollowing his acceptance to a call to the Gospel ministry, Dr. Kevin W. Cosby served as assistant pastor at First Baptist Church in Richmond, Kentucky. In November of 1979, he was called to pastor St. Stephen Baptist Church. He has earned the following degrees: Bachelor of Arts in history from Eastern Kentucky University, Richmond; Master of Divinity from Southern Baptist Theological Seminary, Louisville, Kentucky; and a Doctor of Ministry from United Theological Seminary in Dayton, Ohio.

Dr. Cosby has served as a lecturer at various higher learning facilities, including Bellarmine College, Louisville, Kentucky; DePauw University, Green Castle, Indiana; Kentucky State University, Frankfort, Kentucky; University of Kentucky, Lexington, Kentucky; Greenville College, Greenville, Indiana; Southern Baptist Theological Seminary, Louisville; Presbyterian Theological Seminary, Louisville; University of Tennessee, Knoxville; and Harvard University, Boston, Massachusetts.

Black Baptist Sunday School Growth (Convention Press, 1989), *No Other Help I Know: Sermons on Prayer and Spirituality,* and *The African American Pulpit Series* (Judson Press). In September of 2000, he published his first solo project entitled *Get off Your But!: Messages,*

Musings & Ministries to Empower the African-American Church (Orman Press, 2001). Since then, Dr. Cosby has authored two additional works entitled, *Treasure Worth Seeking* (R. H. Boyd Publishing Corporation, 2003), and *As They Went....* (Christopher Books, 2003).

Dr. Cosby has been featured in the following television programs, magazines, and newspapers:

- "48 Hours" – documentary hosted by Dan Rather
- PBS Special, "The Issue Is Race," hosted by Phil Donahue
- *Jet* magazine
- The Atlanta *Constitution*
- The Baltimore *Sun*
- The Louisville *Courier Journal*
- The Lexington *Herald Leader*
- *Louisville Magazine*, cover story, September 1993 issue
- *Louisville Magazine*, "Highest Ranking African American on the Power List in the City of Louisville," February 1994
- *Leadership Journal*, "Wing Walkers" (Six Key Leaders), Winter 1996
- *Louisville Magazine*, "Ranked in the 2003 Most Powerful/Most Influential List" January 2003 issue
- *Emerge* magazine, featured as "One of Six Super Churches of the South"
- *Business First*, March 1997 and the April 2000 issues.

Additionally, Dr. Cosby has achieved the following:

- Board of Trustees at Kentucky State University
- Former instructor of Pan African Studies at the University of Louisville

- Instructor and mentor for the Cosby-Wheeler Fellows at United Theological Seminary in Dayton, Ohio.

- He has received the WAVE-TV S.T.E.P. (Service Through Excellent Performance) Award

- Regional Minority Business Advocate Award

- Freedom Award, awarded by the mayor of the City of Louisville

- Communicator of the Year Award, awarded by the Kentucky Chapter of the International Association of Business Communicators

- Catholic Alumni Award, presented by the Archdiocese of Louisville.

Dr. Cosby currently serves as adjunct professor, Christian Ministries at the Southern Baptist Theological Seminary.

Under his pastorate at St. Stephen, membership has increased from 500 to over 8,000, and in the process created one of the largest African American Sunday Schools in the South. St. Stephen also became the first African-American church in the state of Kentucky to erect a Family Life Center. In October 2001, a five million dollar expansion of that Family Life Center was completed, which includes a state of the art fitness center.

Presently the campuses of the St. Stephen Church, with its employment of over eighty-five workers, is comprised of:

- Marcus Garvey Place — a reception hall that hosts a multiplicity of local events

- Worship Center — 1,700 seat auditorium that is also used as a cultural arts center

- "A Place For Us" (Pre-school Development Program)

- St. Stephen Academy (before/after school mentoring and tutoring)

- St. Stephen Economic Development Corporation (STEDCO) —building houses in the California Community for low-income families

- Book Link (West Louisville's premiere family bookstore)

- St. Stephen Lifestyle Enrichment Campus (former site of the Simmons University), which offers an array of life skill, nurturing, and recreational programs for individuals and families.

On Easter Sunday 2001, Dr. Cosby planted a new church in the southern Indiana city of Clarksville. Currently worship services are being held at three locations in the metropolitan Louisville area.

Dr. Cosby is married to the former Barnetta Turner and they are the proud parents of two children, Christine and Kevin Christopher.

Printed in the United States
15939LVS00007B/1-72

9 781932 2032